Profitable Model Photography

ART KETCHUM

images
PRESS   INC.

Profitable Model Photography

Library of Congress Catalog Card Number: 91-076494
Art Ketchum
ISBN: 0-929667-12-3

Published by·Images Press, 7 East 17th Street, New York, NY 10003; (212) 675-3707

Printed and bound in the United States of America

Graphic Design and Typography by Ray Noonan, ParaGraphic Artists, New York City

Cover Design by Dawn Daisley

Photographs by Art Ketchum

1 2 3 4 5 6 7 8 9 10

Contents

CHAPTER I

$100 an Hour with Models' Portfolios and Composites

Like most photographers who specialize in model's portfolios and composites, I entered this line of work by the side door. In 1978 I was running a portrait-wedding studio in a Chicago blue collar suburb, a working class neighborhood. And after a year of long hours and hard work, I found that I was not making the kind of money that I wanted and expected. I paid my two employees more than myself and I was not getting any return on the large investment I had in the studio, furnishings and equipment.

Because of the neighborhood, I had a definite ceiling on what I could charge for my wedding and portrait photography and I found I was competing too closely with the Pixie Pinup and K-Mart store shooters with their $12.95 packages. It didn't make any sense to assume the expense of a studio and wear out a Hasselblad every year for $4 a sitting, so I began to look for other ways to make money in photography.

One thing that immediately occurred to me was teaching photography to amateurs. During the time I had run the studio, people had continually come to me with the question, "Why don't you teach photography? You're very good at what you do and I know you would be a good teacher."

If you remember, 1978 is the year Canon introduced the AE-1 and sold millions of them. Suddenly, hordes of people had technically advanced cameras and they all wanted to know how to move from the snapshot level to an

One of my basic classes learning how to dry mount.

My advanced class learns about lighting for small products.

advanced status. So to build additional income for myself, I began to teach photography to all those new owners of fine cameras. The timing was perfect.

I designed a simple five-week course that I taught one night a week and I booked no more than twenty people into any class, figuring that I couldn't handle more than twenty. The class was held in my studio and the students brought their cameras and film so they could photograph the models we had each week. The program began with a thirty minute slide presentation that covered what I wanted to teach that night. Then I brought out the model and took several photographs using a Polaroid back on a Hasselblad, to show in practice what I had illustrated in the slide presentation. After that, the students used their cameras to photograph the model until the end of the class. I was there to answer any questions they had.

I kept it as simple as I could, so simple that I could almost give the program blindfolded. What does the beginning student want to know? He wants to know how to take good pictures of his family and their surroundings and he wants to bring back good photos from his vacation. So, I kept the classes simple and geared toward those two objectives.

Some of the students wanted to jump into complex things like studio lighting from the very beginning and I had to learn to handle that. "Look," I would say, "forget about the complex lighting. For you at this stage of your development as a photographer, there is only light; either the sun, or the flash on your camera. Do everything with one light. If you want to get creative, use fill cards, (sheets of white cardboard), to bounce back some of the sunlight into the faces of your subjects."

I am convinced that too many complications will discourage students. Most of them just want to know how to take better pictures of their families. Teach them that, and you are a success; they will see you as a master teacher.

I charged $55 for the course, so every five weeks I took in $1100 from teaching this basic class, which helped brighten the studio profit picture immensely. Figure it out; twenty students at $55 each, adds up to $1100 every five weeks, which was most welcome at that time and represented a substantial increase in my income. It was virtually 100% profit since the studio overhead was already paid for. All it cost me was two hours of electricity, several sheets of Polaroid film, and a couple of 8 x 10's for the model.

The thing that was different about my classes was that each week I had a different model for them to photograph. At the beginning I used both men and women models, but soon discovered that guys don't care for shooting other men; they want to photograph pretty women. The women students would probably have preferred photographing men, but it didn't seem such a pressing issue to them (and there were fewer women), so I tried to have mostly women as models, except for the times when we photographed children.

About the time the first class was coming to an end, some of the students came to me and asked for an advanced class. I certainly couldn't let that opportunity pass me by. I put together a loosely structured advanced class still based on a five week cycle, but I charged $65 for this one. I called it a workshop and based it upon the interests of the students. It was pretty much an open forum in which a student could bring a magazine or clipping and ask how the picture was made. The students determined the curriculum, which made for great flexibility and lessened my preparation time immensely.

I taught that advanced class for four years and there were people in it who stayed the full four years. Every five weeks they would hand me another check for $65 and we went on with the classes. The advanced class brought in $260 a week and the beginner's class continued to pay off at the rate of $220 a week. I now had an income of more than $1900 a month above the regular studio profits. As you can imagine, I whistled merrily all the way to the bank.

My involvement with photographing models and for money began because of these two classes. When I started the classes, I persuaded friends to act as models in exchange for a couple of prints, and I used a different friend each week. This was okay when there was only the beginner's class, but when the advanced class went on and on, I needed an endless supply of models which I didn't have.

My students regularly told me that one of the attractive things about my classes was that I provided a different model each week. This meant that students could build a varied portfolio of their work. Each class provided a different pose or situation based upon the teaching objective. They wanted those new models and new situations and new set-ups each week, and I was afraid some students would drop out if I could not continue producing new faces for their cameras.

An early ad for my photography classes.

How to get more models? I tried a number of things, including approaching strangers on the street. But finally, I was driven to advertise. I ran a little classified ad in a local shopper newspaper that read:

Immediately the phone began to ring and it didn't stop until more than 200 people had answered that tiny ad. We were totally swamped at the studio and couldn't take care of our regular business. My original plan was to have people come in for a short interview. I would explain that the job was modeling for my classes, that no pay was involved, but the model would be given two 8 x 10 prints that could be used as the beginning of a portfolio.

But the calls came in endlessly and I soon realized that a fifteen minute interview with each person was thirty-two a day. To conduct 200 interviews that way, would take seven days with me functioning as an unpaid instructor and not making one red cent! There had to be a better way.

The better way was to hold a small seminar for would-be models. I ran a second ad and rented a meeting room at a nearby Holiday Inn. All the callers were instructed to come at 5:00 PM on the following Sunday for a two hour mini-seminar on becoming a model. This time I charged for the program (I was learning): $10 for one person, $5 for anyone accompanying the first.

I photographed the covers and contents of various high fashion magazines, plus shots from other magazines, and made up a thirty minute slide show on modeling. I prepared one talk to go with the slides, and another to explain what's involved in becoming a model. I went to several modeling agencies, obtained about fifty composites featuring a variety of different types of models, and made additional slides.

I called the program "Getting Started in Modeling" and it took about two hours to deliver all the material. It was strictly an informational program with no high pressure selling. However, one subtle way to sell is to build confidence in your ability to do what you say you can do. When I showed the composite slides, I did not claim to have made them, but many people assumed that I had. (The fact is, that up to that moment, I had never photographed a model for her portfolio and composite.) I did not intend to deceive anyone, but was just showing composite photography. I would say, "This is a bad composite, and here's why..." or "This is a good composite. Notice this or...."

An ad for my "Get Started in Modeling" seminar.

I explained that a typical model in Chicago earns about $100 an hour (with a two hour minimum), but she rarely earns $4000 a week because her jobs seldom come as forty hour weeks. Even so, if she gets only two jobs a week, for the minimum of two hours, she will make some important money, even a modest living. Some of the women were well supported by husbands or parents, but modeling provided an opportunity for them to make extra money. Perhaps even more important to some, they could now say they were models. To become a model in great demand takes time and talent and not many make it, but it's nice to be known among your friends and relatives as a model.

Models Wanted

ART KETCHUM

PROUDLY PRESENTS A SEMINAR ON

"GETTING STARTED IN MODELING"

THURSDAY, MARCH 31st 1983
6:00 P.M. TO 10:00 P.M.
ELMHURST, HOLIDAY INN

Come and Meet
Jaleigh Jeffers
Miss Illinois—1982

Another ad for my modeling seminar.

After I finished this part of the program, I opened it up to questions. This final part of the program was perhaps the best. I had arranged for two experienced models to answer questions, so I brought them out at this point and let them field the tough ones. They did a good job, answering the questions in a straight-forward manner and explaining what a beginning model could realistically expect.

The first time I did this program I got caught up in the flow of the question-and-answer period and I let it run on too long, so the two-hour program lasted nearly four. Later, I limited the questions to just an hour which was a big improvement.

Forty people showed up for that modeling mini-seminar which meant that I earned nearly $100 an hour for my time. The real payoff, however, came at the end of the program when twenty of them came forward to arrange for photography sessions. I was blown away at the response; half of the entire audience was willing to spend good money for photography and composites!

I thought fifty percent was incredible, but that wasn't the end of it. Over the next several months another twelve people from that group called to say that they were ready to have their photography session. But why hadn't they signed up at the beginning like the others? I asked

Samples of advertising materials I have used in the past.

Models-to-be look at photographs of other models in my "Getting Started in Modeling" seminar.

them and the answer was that even though they had immediately committed themselves to a new career in modeling, they didn't have the money to pay for the photography and composites at that time. They had now saved enough money and were ready to go. The final count was thirty-two out of forty, or an eighty percent positive response!

That was when I realized there was tremendous market for model's photography. There were only a few photographers specializing in it in the greater Chicago area, so I went after it. It didn't take me long to work out the money end of it, either. At that time I made about $300 on a wedding order and it required about thirty two hours of studio personnel time to book the wedding, shoot and deliver it, plus all the negative numbering, ordering and other behind the scenes stuff.

That works out to $10 an hour, while I soon found that I could make nearly $400 from a modeling session on which I rarely spent more than four hours, usually about three to three and a half hours. I could make ten times the money while working one tenth of the time! The sheer potential of a business that paid ten times as well for the time invested was staggering. The only question was whether I could sustain that amount of traffic over the long haul. That question soon answered itself. There is always a new crop of people anxious to become models, so the business is continuous.

That's how it all got started. For a time after that I kept on giving classes in photography and holding modeling mini-seminars, but all the while I nourished a desire to be a commercial photographer. This yen grew and grew until in 1983, I sold my studio in the suburbs and moved into downtown Chicago where I could actively pursue my dream.

I continued to do models' portfolio work while I developed the commercial side of the business and at one point was doing as many as 200 portfolio-composite sessions a year. I netted about $375-$400 from each session, so my income from this one source was $75,000-$80,000 for each year I was willing to sustain the pace. For me, that was several years, but as the commercial side of the business grew, I had to cut back on working with new models until I now average about fifty a year. I never want to stop doing them because they keep me sharp and creative and they are a source of additional commercial business, but one a week is as many as I want to do right now.

When I was still teaching photography, I also held a number of one-shot classes and seminars on a variety of subjects.

CHAPTER II

How Much Can I Make?

The first chapter of this book says you can make $100 an hour photographing models for their portfolios and composites. I have been accused of inflating that figure, but the fact is that I make more than $100. That is not out of line for the Chicago area, but it is a little low for New York or Los Angeles and a little high for much of the rest of the country. Much depends on the demand for models in your part of the world. I also want to make clear that I'm not talking about putting in an eight hour day and being paid $100 for every hour of the day. It means that I make $100+ for every hour I spend with a model and here's how it breaks down.

One thing to keep in mind is your level of expertise in photography. These figures are for an experienced model's photographer. If you are a novice, you cannot charge as much for your work as the fully trained person, but you will still be able to make at least $25 an hour while you're learning. That's pretty good pay for an apprentice.

Okay, here are the figures. First, I charge $225 for the photography session which buys the model my time and the proof sheets. Second, I know I will sell her, on the average, $75 in prints for her portfolio. Third, I sell her composites which I order from a printer who specializes in short-run color printing. The price for this is $250. Fourth, if she is a beginner at modeling, either she or her mother will buy one or more large prints for use at home, although I have not factored this additional sale into the $100 an hour profit.

Let's break this down into hours and dollars and cents. I spend less than three hours on a session with a model during which time I shoot four rolls of film. The cost of the film and processing is about $40. I charge the model $225 for this part of the job, so I "net" $185 for the photography. (I am deliberately omitting the studio overhead and depreciation of the equipment from these calculations as they are adequately compensated for by my commercial work and would only add confusion in this discussion.)

The model will buy five 8 x 10's, either color or b/w, at $15 each. They cost me just $2 each from an inexpensive lab and, although they are not the quality I could get from a custom lab, they are adequate for the model's purpose. (If the model starts to work and stays even slightly busy, she will have replaced these beginning prints with tear sheets or other photos within six months, so they don't have to be great prints. And if she doesn't stay busy, it won't matter, will it?) The profit from five prints at $13 each is $65.

The composites cost me $125 and I double that charge to my customer. She pays $250 and I keep half of that, or $125. Composites are what the agencies send out to their customers to publicize/advertise a model. They are 5 1/2 x 8 1/2 in size and are printed on a ten point card stock (like a picture post card). One side has a big head shot, usually in full color, and the other side has three or four more photos, plus vital statistics, in either color or b/w.

The model will need about 250 of these to start. Most color printers will not work in quantities that small, but, the one I use is Color Q, 2835 Springboro Road, Dayton, OH 45439. Color Q will also work from color prints at no extra charge, so send for a sales kit from them right away.

So what I make is $185 plus $65, plus $125, for a total of $375. I have invested less than three hours of shooting time, a few minutes of telephone time to set up the photo session and the proof-showing appointments, and about twenty to thirty minutes to help the model select the poses for her portfolio and composite. As you can see, I make even a little more than $100 an hour and the extra can go toward studio overhead and equipment depreciation.

There are a few points to consider in the dollars and cents equation. Three hours is the maximum time I spend with a model. I can do the same job for an experienced model in less than two hours, but I have to allow more time for a new model. In fact, I generally have to keep after them to get them out in three

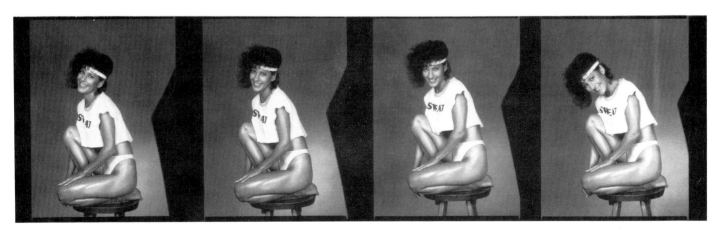

hours. They are slower because everything is so new to them, and they have to be instructed more carefully so that they understand what I want them to do.

Remember, it's all new and exciting and the idea of being a model is a blast and they will want to talk about every aspect of it. You cannot give in to their desire to chatter, or you will find that your three hours has become four or even five. Then she will take half an hour to make the appointment, and an hour and a half to select the poses for the composite. You cannot let her do this. You must take charge and keep tight control of every moment you spend with the model.

The prices I charge for prints may seem cheap to portrait photographers, but remember that these are plain glossy prints that cost me $2 each at Cameo Color. They will be put into a plastic page and discarded in favor of new images in about six months, so who needs retouched, canvas-mounted prints?

As for whether to use a 35mm camera or the Hasselblad, it is pretty much a toss-up. I usually shoot four rolls of film whether I'm using 35mm or 120 and the cost of the film and processing is about $40 with either camera. With the 35mm I have three times as many pictures to show; with the 2 1/4 I probably have just as many good, usable shots because I take more time and work more carefully when I shoot the larger format film. I get more spontaneity with the 35mm, but I get better quality with the 2 1/4. For the normal model's session I use the 35mm, but if I think I may want to make big prints for my wall, or if I perceive that the model will probably order large prints for herself, I reach for the Hasselblad so that I can make them as big as I want.

How do I know that a model may want big prints for herself? I can usually tell during the pre-session consultation (usually on the phone). When I tell her this will cost her about $600 and she says, "Oh, that's okay," I am pretty sure money is not a problem in her household, and she will buy larger prints if I suggest them. If she buys larger prints, my hourly profits take a good, healthy jump. I'm sure you know I don't mind that at all.

There is also something called "selling" that can up your averages by quite a few dollars. I know one man who sells his way to a Hawaiian vacation every year. He puts the profit from every extra picture he sells into his vacation fund, and he averages two extra prints sold per session. If his prices are the same as mine and if he does as many sittings as I did at my peak, the two prints that

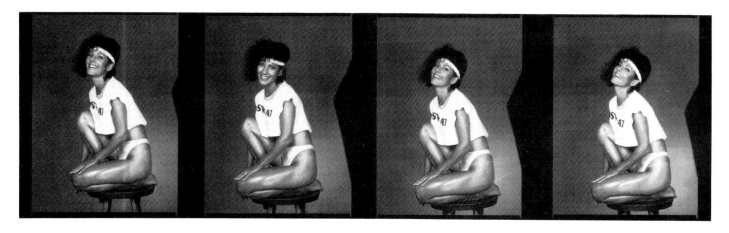

cost him $4 he sells for $30, for a net of $26. Multiply the $26 by 200 sittings and you have $5200. That will buy a month's stay for his family at a classy condo on the beach—a very nice way to spend his Januarys. There's enough extra money so that his wife doesn't have to cook a single meal, unless she wants to, and they can go dancing every night.

If you like that idea (although you may prefer Majorca, the Virgin Islands or Guadalajara to Hawaii), just do a little selling when you show the proofs. Here's the way I do it and so can you. When the model comes in to see the sheets of proofs, you should have four set-ups to show from. That limits the number of additional poses you can sell, so what I do is suggest that she use two prints of each set-up in her portfolio, plus one pose on her composite, for a total of three shots from each set-up. That brings the total to twelve. Since she needs only five shots for her composite, she will have seven pictures more than she needs as the minimum starter package. That is good for her if the poses are varied enough, and is also good for your vacation fund.

The truth is that I rarely sell a dozen pictures to a beginner, but I can almost always find a couple of extra poses that she wants for her portfolio. This is the simplest sort of suggestive selling, just plant the idea and let her sell herself. But, to do this, you have to show proofs that give her the opportunity to buy more than one pose. That is why it's important to take verticals and horizontols of each outfit. If you photograph them properly, the outfits will look different in each pose and give her more to choose from.

Once in a great while a girl will come in, look at the first proof sheet (which is of a single set-up) and order five photos from that one sheet. Then she'll look at the next sheet and order four or five from it, then do the same with the next sheet and the last one, too. Nothing larger than an 8 x 10 and nothing smaller—unless she wants a wallet for the boyfriend.

You may be thinking that there are easier ways to make money in photography, ways where you will work less and make more, but I have done most of the other things and I know there is no easier money to be made in photography. Many photographers get started in professional photography doing weddings, either for studios or for themselves. It may seem that you could do as well with weddings as with model's portfolios, but my experience as a studio owner was that my staff and I put in at least thirty hours on each wedding. That includes

Here I am using the technique of "selling up" through suggestion.

not only the photography time, but all the other time that has to be invested when you do weddings.

I averaged about $300 "profit" from each wedding, so the hourly rate was only $10. That's less than a ditch digger makes, and he has none of the responsibility that falls on a photographer of weddings. Frankly, I am much happier making $100 an hour with models than just $10 hourly with nervous, twitchy brides and their pushy mothers.

So, you see that $100 an hour is not pie-in-the-sky in the sweet-bye-and-bye, but is something you can earn and enjoy as soon as you are able to produce the quality photographs the models and their agencies are looking for. That need not be more than a couple of months from now. Are you ready?

CHAPTER III

Fulfilling Her Dream

A woman who comes to me saying she wants to be a model may have one or more motivations. She may be conscious of some of them, but often she is not even aware of them. In any case, they are all part of her dream of being a model and I intend to help her fulfill as many of them as I can.

Here are some observations from a man who has been professionally involved with photographing models and would-be models for more than ten years.

The first type of woman who says, "I want to be a model," is one who seriously intends to make a career of modeling or who will give it her best shot. She has seriously evaluated her potential for success in this field and she believes that she has the temperament as well as the physical qualifications to do the job. Very often she has set goals and allotted a time to reach them, and this is the one who is most likely to succeed in achieving her dream of actually being a model.

There is a second type of woman whose modeling dream is to be *thought of* as a model, to have her friends believe that she's a model. The woman who is the ultimate manifestation of this, always carries some of her composites in her purse so she can produce them on demand to prove that she is a model. The normal scenario is that she meets a guy in a bar and he asks what she does for a living.

"I'm a model," she chirps, but he knows that even prostitutes pass themselves off as models, so he says, "No, what do you *really* do?"

"I'm really a model," she replies. "Here, look at this." She produces her composite and "proves" that she is actually a model.

For her, being known as a model is enough of a dream. To become a model, in reality, involves a lot of hard work. How much better, she thinks, to have the reputation of a model with none of the labor required to actually become one. That is why she's willing to spend hundreds of dollars to achieve her dream.

The third type of "model" is the one who dreams of being a model, but is unwilling to put forth the effort. She is different from the second type however, in that she's willing to work in front of a camera as a model, but only if it comes to her easily or is thrust on her by a cooperative Fate. She is very much like the woman who came to the famed pianist after a concert and gushed, "Oh, Mr. Horowitz, I'd give *anything* to be able to play like that!" His answer was, "No, you wouldn't; there's too much work involved."

In the same way, many women who dream of being models are like people who dream of being great photographers, painters, furniture makers, or anything else that takes time, effort and much, much practice to attain. All of us to some extent want to be Someone or Something, but most of us settle for far less because we aren't willing to put out the effort it takes to be the best. It takes years of training and concentration to be an Olympic champion or a prima ballerina or the next Ansel Adams: if you're not willing to expend great effort over the many years it takes to become the best, then you're only dreaming.

There are other reasons for women to pursue the dream of being a model, but they are not so apparent and we don't need to look into them here. The reason I have gone into this is so you will realize that some of the women who come to you for help in reaching their modeling goals will never go beyond having their photographs taken and the composites made. A few will go so far as to take their comps to one or more agencies, but not many.

The tigers will call on all the talent agencies, then begin with ad agency art directors, large department store advertising departments and commercial photographers. A few will even go so far as to call on merchants and manufacturers who use models in their advertising. These are the ones who will not be stopped and who will find lots of work as models.

So what do you do about those whom you recognize as being less than totally dedicated to the profession of modeling? Do you turn them down and say, "I perceive that you're not really serious about a career in modeling so I won't do your photos?" Of course not. Your job is not to judge why she wants those pictures and composites; your job is to make the very best photographs you can and leave the rest up to her. Fulfilling her dreams is not your responsibility.

But what if a woman wants to be a model (and she's dead serious about it), but lacks the physical qualifications. She has a plain face, a dumpy body and a muddy complexion. Should you tell her, "Sorry, honey, you don't have a chance to get even one job as a model. You are totally lacking in what it takes, etc." Of course not! Your job is to help her fulfill the dream, not smash it. Besides, if you refuse her, she probably won't believe you and will go to another photographer, one who understands that she has a need (that may not be apparent to you) to fulfill this dream, even though it has nothing to do with modeling.

You will photograph her to the best of your ability and with all the skills you and your makeup artist can bring to the job. You will give her the very best job you are capable of and you may be surprised at the results. Remember, anyone can take an outstanding picture if the model is one of New York's finest $1000-a-day posers, so where's the pride in doing that? But the person who can

photograph Ms. Jane Plain so she looks the very best she can is the skilled workman.

And never forget that Jane's friends know what she really looks like, so when they see the great shots you got of her, many of them will come to you for their photographs. What happens is that Jane's friends had no previous thought of modeling, but when Jane the Plain announces that she's now a model and flashes her photos and comps, many of them will say, "If Jane can be a model, how much easier for me to be one, too, because I'm better looking by far."

If these women are even half-smart, they will ask who Jane's photographer is because you're absolutely a miracle worker and they want the best, too. So, good photography for Jane Plain means that you get jobs from prettier women who are easier to photograph, and who look better in the finished photos. Doing an honest job for Jane will bring you more and more business, and by forcing you to the limits of your skills, it will also make you a better photographer, much more qualified to get the good jobs that are now going to the top photographers. That's the real pay-off and it is one reason why I can now bid on and get good-paying commercial work.

What's the first question a new model asks when she comes to me for photography? It's, "Do you think I can make it as a model?" It doesn't matter if she is a great beauty or Jane Plain, every one of them asks the same question. She knows that I have photographed many of the top models in Chicago, plus other outstanding beauties such as Playboy Playmates and beauty queens, so she figures I'm an expert and can evaluate her chances in the open market.

My answer is always, "Of course, you can make it as a model (even if she's only five feet tall and twenty pounds overweight), but it's going to take a lot of work, real hard work." And she always replies, "Oh, I don't mind hard work."

They always tell you they're willing to work hard, but hard work alone just won't cut it and six months down the road most of them will have given up. Some of these may whine about not having friends in the right places, but I suspect that most of them realize they just don't have what it takes. They were living a dream.

They have to have some luck, sometimes a lot of it, to succeed as models. It's a little like the odds against winning in the state lottery. If you shoot craps at Vegas or Atlantic City, the house has an advantage of a few percentage points, but a dash of luck can overcome that advantage. The lottery, however,

typically gives you only one chance in about seven to win *anything*, while the odds of winning one of the big money prizes are on the order of millions-to-one against you. The odds against success in modeling aren't that bad if you're young, tall and pretty, but for anyone else the odds are pretty horrible.

I know right up front that most of the women who come to me will not succeed in getting more than an occasional job as models, even many of the real beauties. So am I lying to them when I speak of "real hard work"? No, because I know several women who are not terribly pretty, just ordinary looking women with ordinary figures, who have successfully modeled for four or five years. Are they making big bucks? Probably not, but they are paying the rent and their other living expenses, making more than enough to get by on, all from what they earn as models.

I don't know about this girl, but if she has the drive and the willingness to do what she must, she, like so many before her, can find work as a model and make a living at it. This is not to say she will be a smash success at it (although that's possible, too), but that she can make a modest living doing the marginal types of modeling.

Knowing this, I am not going to play God and tell any woman that she can't make it as a model and that she's wasting her time and money. I don't have the heart for it. Besides, if I burst her bubble, she may hate me for doing so, but she'll probably still go ahead and have her pictures done by another photographer who won't do as well by her.

The amazing thing is that while beauty alone may be enough for certain types of modeling where the model is just a clothesrack, most modeling calls more for personality than for looks. If a woman has a good personality, projects well, strives to get along with her co-workers, and is an outgoing, fun person, she will do far better in modeling than if she is an introvert. The introvert has two strikes against her, unless she has a "stage mother" dragging her from photographer to talent agency to interview.

Brooke Shields, for instance, didn't make it on her own, but because of her mother's relentless pursuit of a career in modeling for her. Shields has a beautiful face perched atop the figure of a tall, lanky man—straight up and down—plus eyebrows Michael Dukakis might envy. If she had come along a couple of years earlier, it's a cinch her agency would have made her pluck and prune those

bushy 'brows. But her timing was right on and the arbiters of fashion said, "Hey, a new thing!"

I have no compunction at all about helping women fulfill their fantasies of modeling because I perform a very real and valuable service they may not be able to get elsewhere. I feel quite justified in taking their $600. Most of the marginal women know, deep down, that if they went to a talent agency first, they would be turned down. But, they recognize that a photographer has a commercial interest in producing what they want, so a give-and-take relationship springs up between us. I help her fulfill her fantasy and she pays me well for doing it.

There are several reasons why I don't want to shatter her dreams. The main one is that if I don't do her photographs, another photographer will. There are few of them who will empathize as much with her yearnings as I will, and fewer still who will give the quality photography I will. If she's going to spend her $600, she will be better off, in most cases, having me do the photography and so will I.

Many women think that to be a model, it's good to start off by going to modeling school. This is not so. In fact, modeling schools are more often counter-productive than otherwise. Doctors can learn the rudiments of medicine in school, but they then spend several years doing residency to learn the rest of their trade. If a woman starts out by going to a modeling school, she may have to spend a two-year residency UN-learning what she was taught in the school, which constitutes a big and expensive waste of time.

The truth about modeling schools is that they will take anyone as a student, even those who obviously have no chance to succeed. They will hand the same spiel to a very plain girl of 5'2" and 150 pounds as they do to a lanky beanpole with a beautiful face. (Don't I do the same? No, because I don't PERsuade the women to come to me, I just don't DISsuade those who are already embarked on a career move toward modeling.)

Most modeling schools have a single (money-making) function. They serve as cheap finishing schools that mothers send their daughters to for some of the polish and confidence they didn't get at home and to help them blossom into young women who can hold their own in a social situation. The moms pay a pretty high price for what they get—their daughters' ability to walk and stand gracefully and do other things they should have learned in the growing up process.

The problem for women who hope to use a modeling school to prepare for a career change is that the schools can not really teach them to move or pose as a model should. They teach stock poses, (the agencies call them "freeze poses"), which are dull and stereotyped and are no longer used by anyone except the schools.

Makeup application is most often taught to the incoming students by a graduate of the last class and is a case of the blind leading the blind. What is taught might look good on a sixty year old woman, but it's usually hard, brassy and dated, often looking like it was put on with a plasterers' trowel instead of a brush. If I know one of my customers is coming right out of modeling school, I ask her to come in without makeup so she can have a professional make-over by my staff person.

If she comes from modeling school, I know that I am in trouble not only with her makeup, but also with her posing and probably her looks. Most grads of modeling schools are not pretty enough to hack it out in the commercial world of modeling, although many of them could go out as character models.

There is one good thing about modeling schools, however, that can work to your advantage. If you can get into these schools as an expert speaker, you will find that many of the students will come to you for photography. Most of the schools have an arrangement with one or more photographers who pay a kickback or have their fee built into the school's costs. Despite this, if you come in as an outside speaker (which can happen as soon as you have compiled a few credits working with models), you will find a steady trickle of business coming to you from each school you speak at. The students who are serious about a career in modeling will come to you for additional photography because the photos done by the school's captive cameraman are never enough and they are often of recognizably poor quality. You will show the quality of your photography when you speak at the school, so the girls are primed to come to you when they want more.

I have gotten a lot of business from modeling schools without becoming one of their captive cameramen. You can do the same.

Another good thing about modeling schools when you are starting out is that they are a good source of models on whom you can practice your photography and hone your posing skills. But, you should only use the girls who are in the

final phases of their course. By then they have some photos on file at the school so you can make a preliminary selection of a model to work with before you actually see her.

Don't expect too much from these poorly-taught beginners and you'll not be too disappointed, but you will learn very rapidly how to work with amateur models and get good poses and expressions. You will learn how to direct them with your voice only (Look, Ma, no hands!) and how to direct what you want them to do in a clear decisive manner. When you finish working with several dozens of these students, you should be well on your way toward being a skillful director and photographer of models.

One thing to watch out for with these people, however, is that they will begin to haunt you for testing sessions, if you allow it to happen. Once they see that you are trying to perfect your skills with models and that you're doing better and better work, many of them will come to you and ask if you'd like to test with them.

"Testing" is a long-standing tradition with models and photographers and it simply means that the photographer and the model work together to carry out an idea one of them has to their mutual benefit. Let's say you see a shot in a magazine that you like, but are not sure how it was done. You call in a model you know and ask her to test with you so you can learn this technique and perhaps have a new picture for the portfolios of both of you. The model comes in and poses while you work out the pose, lighting, or whatever. She doesn't charge for her time and you don't charge for yours, but she gets a free print of each pose you worked on together and you have some new knowledge and skills, so both of you benefit. That's the simple story of testing.

The problem that arises with girls from modeling schools who want to test is that they rarely bring you any intriguing new ideas to work on that will make you a better, sharper photographer. They just want to add some free pictures to their portfolios and they like your work, so here they come.

However, you can develop some business from testing with modeling school students. When the girls you have worked with show off their proof-sheets and finished photos at the schools, many of their classmates will come to you for additional photos, so you'll make out okay.

Even so, when I get a call from one of these young women who want to test, I say, "Sure, I'd like to test with you, but I charge for testing." That's usually the end of that discussion. If, however, you find the girl who wants to test is a real bona fide beauty and you really want to photograph her, you can always make an exception. Naturally!

There's another good reason for testing and that's so you can make a presentation to an art director in connection with an account you are going after. For instance, one local department store chain runs full page ads for their fashion department that feature lovely, vibrant young women doing things like running, jumping rope or doing dance steps. They are totally different from the stereotypical languid beauty who lolls through the pages of Vogue and for that reason they are distinctive and very attractive.

I wanted to land that account, so I reasoned that if I could produce photographs that were similar in appearance and feel, but with that Art

Ketchum touch, the account would be mine. So, I found out who the models were who were being featured at that time in these ads, called and told them what I wanted to do and arranged to test with them.

I did the shots, made up the prints and carried them to the art director. He like them so well that the account became mine on the spot. He later told me that he was most impressed with the way I had gone after the account and wondered why more photographers did not do the same. I know that I'm not the only photographer in Chicago who can think this way, so I know I must be on my toes to keep the account, but that's the sort of thing that keeps me sharp.

CHAPTER IV

Types of Models

When you hear the word "model", what image comes to your mind? If you're like most of us, the first thing you visualize is a tall, arrogant beauty who appears in Vogue or Elle and wears the latest fashions from Chanel or Dior. It is true that some models are exactly like that, but there are far more who make a good living posing for photographs for more mundane magazines or working in television.

Think for a moment about Maytag's lonely repairman or Mikey who eats the new cereal his brothers are suspicious of ("He likes it! He likes it!"), or the woman who uses Midol, Tide or Pinesol. Every one of these is a model just as surely as the tall skinnybones in Harper's Bazaar, and some of them make a lot of money doing every day or silly things. What's a lot of money? How about $100,000 or $250,000 a year? That's what some of the top TV models make when the residuals are added in, and that's a living in any league.

When the average woman decides to be a model, what she wants most is to be that woman on the cover of Vogue. She doesn't understand that no one can model fashions unless she's 5'6" tall and she cannot do HIGH fashion unless she's about 5'9". She may be utterly gorgeous, with the greatest shape since Marilyn Monroe, but if she's only five feet two, she can never be a fashion model.

Does that mean all modeling doors are closed to her? No, it only means that she can't be a fashion model. Unfortunately, when most women decide to pursue a career in modeling, fashion is all they can think of and that's too bad. A pretty woman who is shorter can have a great career in modeling,

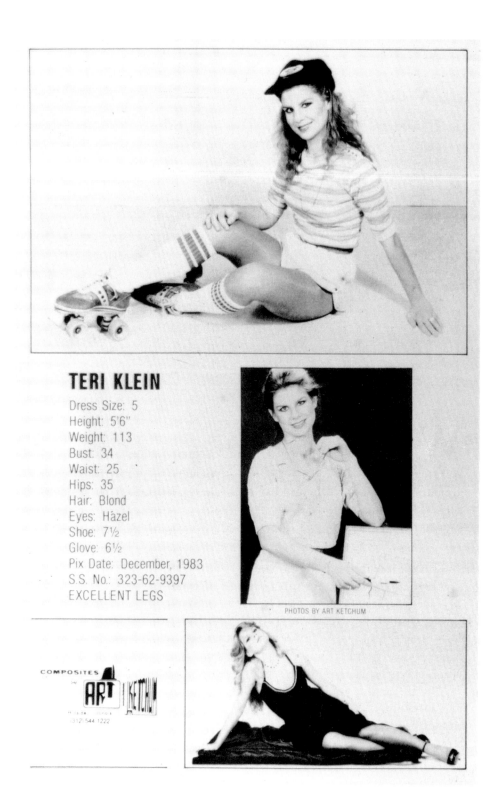

TERI KLEIN

Dress Size: 5
Height: 5'6"
Weight: 113
Bust: 34
Waist: 25
Hips: 35
Hair: Blond
Eyes: Hazel
Shoe: 7½
Glove: 6½
Pix Date: December, 1983
S.S. No.: 323-62-9397
EXCELLENT LEGS

PHOTOS BY ART KETCHUM

COMPOSITES ART KETCHUM
(312) 544-1222

A typical young model. Notice the date on the composite, important with young models who change so rapidly. The last is also important because the excellence of her legs is not fully shown in these photos.

Marketers wanting to penetrate the black market must use black models in at least some of their advertising. This girl's great smile will help her to succeed as a model.

Gina is another young girl who may find plenty of work because of her diminutive size.

GINA

Gina Gabriel

Dress Size: 3   Height: 5'2"   Weight: 101
Bust: 33   Waist: 24   Hips: 33
Hair: Brunette   Eyes: Hazel   Shoe: 7½
Pix Date: Dec., 1983   S.S. No.: 329-42-9853
Talents: Acting

OTHER IMAGES PRESS BOOKS OF INTEREST

ACHIEVING PHOTOGRAPHIC STYLE. *By Michael Freeman.* A fascinating exploration into the aesthetic qualities that make a photograph great, this book will challenge the reader to think carefully about the creation of your photographic images. Illustrated by leading photographers. 224pp. 8½ x 11   **ONLY $21.95**

HOW TO BUILD YOUR OWN PHOTOGRAPHIC EQUIPMENT. *by Dan Lewis.* Complete instructions for the photographer who wishes to save money and custom make popular accessories. contains over 75 plans for useful items for lighting, darkroom, close-up work, print finishing, and viewing transpariencies. 144pp. 8½ x 11   **ONLY $19.95**

HOW TO START AND RUN A SUCCESSFUL PHOTOGRAPHY BUSINESS. *By Gerry Kopelow.* Fascinating, complete guide to setting up a photography business. Pricing, promotion, processing, computers, much more. Great advice! 160pp.   **ONLY $19.95**

PHOTO BEST SELLERS. Best selling stock photos that have earned one agency's photographers over two million dollars in sales. Actual sales records and ideas for the photographer looking for inspiration. 9¼ x 12.   **Originally $29.95 SPECIAL $14.95**

SUCCESSFUL FINE ART PHOTOGRAPHY. *By Harold Davis.* Practical, in-depth guide to marketing photographic prints. Interviews with leading photo art dealers and photographers. Resource section with names, addresses, and phone numbers of sales contacts. B/W& color photos. 176pp. 8½ x 11.   **ONLY $21.95**

THE PHOTO GALLERY AND WORKSHOP HANDBOOK. *By Jeff Cason.* U.S. & International gallery guide and workshop directory. Detailed listings, interviews with gallery and workshop directors, photo investing price guides of collectible photo art, auctions, and how to present your photographs to galleries.   **ONLY $19.95**

THE PHOTOMARKETING HANDBOOK - THIRD EDITION. *By Jeff Cason.* Included in this volume: detailed market listings, of publishers, paper product companies, domestic and foreign agencies, telling you exactly what editors and agents are looking for. In depth profiles with professional photographers, editors, and agents telling you what it takes to succeed. Sample business forms, photographer-agency agreement, and book publishing contracts. Newspaper listings worldwide. Reproduction fee chart. Color pages from photo agency catalogs worldwide. 302pp. 8½ x 11.   **ONLY $21.95**

NIKON SYSTEM HANDBOOK. *By B. Moose Peterson.* Complete Nikon guide to current and older models. Lens production and comprehensive discussion of all Nikkor SLR lenses produced. Illustrated guide to complete Nikon system, including accessories. Includes price guide to all bodies and lenses.   **ONLY $19.95**

PROFITABLE MODEL PHOTOGRAPHY. *By Art Ketchum.* All you need to know to get started and manage a successful model photography studio! Build a profitable business photographng model portfolios and composites. Included in ths photo-packed volume: Advice on lab services and keeping processing costs down. Information on backgounds, locations, and props. Lighting advice including flash and fill-flash. Discovering the secrets of posing and directing models. Advertising, promotion, and pricing your work. And more!   **ONLY $18.95**

PHOTOGRAPHER'S PUBLISHING HANDBOOK. *By Harold Davis.* Comprehensive references on all aspects of publishing photographic imagery including photo books and paper products. Included in this volume are instructions on how to: create publishable imagery. Publish self-promotion pieces. Market stock photos to publishers. Self-publish. Create a reputation as a photographer.   **ONLY $19.95**

We Need Your Help!

Images Press books are successful because of readers like you. Would you please help us continue the dialog? Your comments and suggestions help us improve our books and let us know what you are interested in reading and learning about. Please take a moment to fill in and return the postcard below and we'll send you a complimentary copy of our latest book catalog.

We hope you enjoy the **PROFITABLE MODEL PHOTOGRAPHY** and find it a useful addition to your library. Your comments and suggestions would be greatly appreciated.

Your comments: _____
_____
_____
_____
_____
_____

Please return this card for a complementary photo/book catalog from IMAGES PRESS.

Name _____
                                                      Please Print
Address _____
City _____ State _____ Zip _____
Country _____

BUSINESS REPLY MAIL
FIRST CLASS   PERMIT NO. 337   NEWARK, NJ

Postage will be paid by

IMAGES PRESS
7 East 17th Street
New York NY 10003-1995

SAMANTHA

Samantha Slade

Dress Size: 5/6
Height: 42"
Weight: 39 lbs.
Hair: Blond
Eyes: Blue
Pix Date: Oct., 1983
S.S. #: 340-72-5547
D.O.B.: 8-4-78

COMPOSITES
by ART KETCHAM
Hillside   Illinois
(312) 544-1222

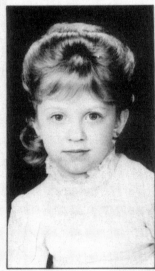

earning $1000 or more weekly, even if she's too short to make the fashion scene. The trick is to convince her not to chase that dream, but to go after the much more realizable dream of selling stuff on TV or being photographed for Popular Mechanics or Family Circle magazine.

If a model comes to me before she has been to a talent agency, she doesn't really know what she is capable of doing. She may think of herself as high fashion, while she actually looks like a cute kitten of a high school girl. If I see that she has not really thought through her appearance and basic look, I will talk to her like she was my own daughter and explain what the real modeling world out there is like.

If she accepts what I say, that's great and we work from there to present her in the best possible way. But if she insists she wants to look like the Vogue cover woman, what should I do? The only thing I can do is present her exactly the way she wants to be presented, as a high fashion model. She's the one paying for it and she has the right to insist that I photograph her exactly the way she wants to be presented. It's what happens afterward that I cannot control.

Let's assume that Daddy is staking his precious daughter in her pursuit of a modeling career. She's fresh out of high school, perhaps has a year of college, and she has the modeling bug. She prevails on Good Old Dad to buy her pix and composites and support her until she begins to earn some modeling bucks. He's agreeable to it because that's what his Baby wants and it surely won't cost as much as sending her to college.

So she comes to me for a set of photographs that will make her look like the cover of Vogue. She is very pretty, with nice hair and figure, she handles herself well and everything looks great for her, except she's only 5'4".

So I go to work on her, explaining that there is no way she can make it as a high fashion model unless she knows how to add four or five inches to her height. But high fashion is what she wants to do and that's the way she wants to be presented. Besides, what other kind of modeling is there?

So I begin to explain all the other types, explaining about character modeling, TV work, and the marvelous residuals that go with it, magazine work that is not high fashion, and so on. In the end, she may accept what I am saying or she may not. If I can get Dad into the act, I know my chances of getting my way are much better because he can grasp what I'm driving at without the emotional hang-ups about fashion she has generated.

But what happens if I lose and have to present her as the ultimate clothesrack? That will be the end of her modeling career. When the talent agencies compare the sleek image on the composites with the very pretty, but short reality, they may send her back to start over from scratch to get a new set of photos made according to their specs. But that doesn't happen often enough to mention.

Do you want to sell a new chewing gum? You wouldn't ask Bartles and Jaymes to pitch it for you, would you? No, you'd look for some fresh young high school

kids to bounce and prance through your commercial, dancing to rock or horsing around at the beach. You'd probably look for someone just like this young girl. That's the spot you should aim her for, and with a little luck, she'll find work in that slot and keep busy at it.

As you can see, she should exploit her youthful freshness and vivacity to get the modeling jobs that a thirty year old looks right in. She's part of the Pepsi generation, so stick a Pepsi in her hand and shoot her smiling her toothimost at the camera. That's a natural for her.

What is unnatural for her? Think about it for a moment; what sort of women model what sorts of things? The women who model Blackglama minks, for instance, are all in their thirties, forties and fifties. Women who have succeeded in their careers, all of them seeming to be supremely confident of their own "glama" and cachet. Can you visualize this eighteen year old girl who has done nothing more noteworthy than be a high school cheerleader wearing a Blackglama mink?

And what kind of car would you use her to sell? A Rolls, a Mercedes Benz or a Jaguar? Hardly! Maybe you'd put her in a Mustang, but probably in a Ford Escort, a Dodge Omni or a Yugo, the kind of first wheels Dads buy for daughters. That is realism; it sells cars and fits her image perfectly.

Now think about the woman who pitches Tide detergent on TV. Is that the same sort of woman who wears Blackglama mink or drives a Bentley? Never! She looks like the woman who lives a few doors down the street, but maybe a little prettier. She wears a house dress or a pair of jeans and she may have her hair wrapped in a dish towel to keep the dust out of it. She's your neighbor and that's the person you trust to tell you about a great new product she just tried.

In a few years, your high school girl can move up to the young housewife image and sell breakfast cereals. If she keeps her figure trim, later she can be the mother of a teenager and eventually she can learn to bellow out, "Where's the beef?" It's just a question of making her fit into the image people will have of her because of her age, size and other factors.

This type of modeling is called "character" modeling, and good character models can go on forever. This is especially true if you get an ongoing character part such as the Maytag repairman. He has been around for maybe ten years, looking mournful because no one ever brings a Maytag in for repairs. In actual fact, he probably smiles continuously as he considers his career with Maytag which must be worth at least a quarter million to him every year. Those residuals add up, you know.

Almost any modeling except fashion is called character modeling and it is what most people do who work as models. The demand for people who can realistically portray "characters" is much greater than for high fashion modeling. And that's why I never discourage even women who look like Ruth Bussey on the park bench. There is a spot for just about everyone who wants one badly enough.

If the woman goes with the part or character I am trying to establish for

Perfect eyes, hands, or feet can mean big bucks for the right woman in advertising.

her, I will present her in a variety of situations that will sell her in exactly the way the agencies will like. This may involve set-ups that do not make her look good, but which will sell her perfectly to the agencies and their clients. I'm not boasting; I can do precisely that time after time. For instance, more than once I have ended a session by having the woman soap up her hair as for a shampoo ad. These will be the last shots of the day and she rinses her hair and leaves.

If she's pretty and has outstanding eyes, you can position her for eye makeup ads and Maybelline alone could keep her busy. If she has beautiful, slender hands—a real rarity—she can pose for gloves, jewelry ads and hand lotions.

Her face may never appear in a single ad, but she can work steadily at her specialty and make an excellent income.

This is also true of the woman who has a size five foot attached to a shapely ankle and calf. A woman's size five foot is the precise size to display shoes in perfect proportion. The woman who has one can work all day, every day until she drops dead. She'll make a lot of money for as long as she wants to work and never once have to make up her face.

Great legs are always an asset, so if you get a leggy one in the studio, be sure to feature the stems in her photographs. Long, slender legs are valuable and they should be highlighted in at least one of her composite photos.

With the model's cooperation I do whatever is necessary to get her new career off on the right foot. She is obviously making a career move as she leaves her current work and goes into modeling. She's probably bored with what she does and wants to get into work she sees as exciting and glamorous.

But, you ask, won't she be bored with modeling, too, in a few months or a year? I have never met anyone who was. I have never heard a person returning from a modeling job say, "This is such boring work, really terrible, that I have to get out of it." People don't leave this industry. Once in it they stay until they're no longer wanted.

As I write this I'm reminded to say that a tall, heavy woman can find work modeling fashions, at least sporadically, in certain catalogs such as Roaman's or Lane Bryant, which are aimed at large women. It is also possible that a smaller woman of the right age can model junior and petite fashions, and so might find a temporary career in that niche of the fashion market.

The smaller woman must realize that it's not her image of herself that will get her work, but the image the industry has of her. If she's a neat petite, there's no way she'll ever appear on the cover of Vogue or Elle, but she can stay forever busy selling soap or tennies or sweat shirts or almost anything but fashions.

She might look great using Ivory dishwashing liquid with a smudge on her perky little nose; selling the latest shampoo with her hair all sudsy and smiling at the camera; or telling her dumb husband why he should take Anacin Plus for his cold. But if she doesn't yet see herself doing any of those things, she'll be convinced you want to turn her into a frump rather than bring out her beauty. Because she wants to be beautiful in her photos, it's difficult to sell her on being a "character", but that's what you have to do. If you do it correctly, you'll be well paid for your trouble.

CHAPTER V

Model's Composites and Actor's Glossies

Models use composites, actors use glossies. The difference is this: a composite is a product of a printer's press, while the actors' glossies are made on photographic paper in a darkroom.

Composites have changed over the years, but at this time they are usually 5 1/2 x 8 inches, printed on ten point card stock (the same as a picture post card). Most often there is a full color photo on the front and three or four b/w's on the back. The front photo is almost always a head shot and it can also be b/w for economy's sake, but the saving is small, hardly worth it. In addition to the photos on the comp there is a list of the model's sizes that reads something like this: Height: 5'7", Weight: 115 lbs., Bust: 34", Waist: 25", Hips: 35", Size: 5–7, Hair: Lt. Brown, Eyes: Blue. If she has other special qualifications that make her especially attractive for some purpose, those will be listed too. A good example is "shoe size 5", because that is the perfect size for showing shoes to their best advantage. A woman with a size five foot and a trim ankle on the end of an attractive calf can work every day for fifty-two weeks a year until her arches fall and the varicose veins pop out like a boa constrictors.

Sometimes the composite bears the line, "Pix taken (date)." This is usually done with kids because they change so fast. It could be very embarrassing to put in a call for a four year old child and discover the composite pix were taken a year or two earlier and are totally unlike the child today.

Mary Kay ...

Mary Kay Moss

Dress Size: 5-7
Height: 5'6"
Weight: 107
Bust: 34
Waist: 24
Hips: 34
Hair: Auburn
Eyes: Brown
Shoe: 7½-8
Pix Date: Dec., 1983
S.S. #
  320-50-4275

The usual procedure is to have a big head on the front of a composite. This one does not, but look at the impact of this photo: it comes from the pose, the clothes, the bare shoulder and feet, and the direct look and smile. It certainly succeeds in grabbing attention, which is the object of the comp.

Pam Pawlak

The front of a composite has a big head on it; the back has three or four other looks—all different—plus the vital statistics of the model.

At one time, composites were printed on 8 1/2 x ll, but that is now passe. Occasionally a model will want to make a bigger impression, so she will make her composite the larger size, perhaps with color on both sides but fold it in the middle so that it measures just 5 1/2 x 8 1/2 when it is finished. This can be very effective if it's well done.

Sometimes a model gets into a new look and she (or the agency she works with) wants to add that look to her composite. Unfortunately, if she still has 200 of the old comps left, she won't want to throw them out because they are expensive. In this case, she will often add a glossy to the package, the glossy illustrating the new look. This is usually shot as a one roll job by the photographer and it is printed up as a 5 x 7/5 x 8 glossy because that size can be mailed in the same envelope as the slightly larger composite. This may be in color, but is usually b/w.

Some beginning models use a glossy as a half-hearted try to test the waters of modeling without spending the money for a full composite, but this is a mistake. The glossies don't have the impact on the ad agencies that the composites do.

The four or five photographs on the composite should illustrate the different looks the model can project. It should never contain more than one shot of the model in a given outfit, although the big, tight head shot on the front will be the exception. The costume, however, hardly shows in a tight head shot; the big head supplies the impact.

Jill Dellert

Height: 5'7"	Dress Size: 5
Weight: 115 ·	Hair: Auburn
Bust: 34	Eyes: Blue
Waist: 24	Shoe: 7½
Hips: 34	Glove: 7½

Pix Date: 2/84
S.S. No.: 346-68-1635
Talents: Dance

There are two ways to create a composite. First, the agency and the model work together to select the looks and the photographs that will go on it. Second, the model and her photographer work as a team to create a strong statement that will sell the model.

Most inexperienced models who come to me do not have an agency helping them, so they expect me to guide them in the photography and composite. I not only help them do this, but I also steer her toward the agencies that I believe can best represent her. No agency will list her if they don't think they can sell her to their clients, so I try to match up the new model with an agency that will work hard for her. I want "my" models to succeed.

There are seventeen talent agencies in Chicago at this time and, of those seventeen, perhaps five or six will list a new model. If she has a lot going for her, that number may jump to as many as ten. The agency must believe the model will be a marketable commodity for them, or they won't list her. When she goes into their stable, they ask for composites. The comps are then sent out to advertising agencies, department stores, photographers who are known to use models regularly, all the different places where this new person may find work.

From this initial exposure to the trade, the model may get some calls. But because she hasn't done any modeling before, the calls won't be for modeling jobs, just for interviews. She isn't paid for this, but she gets a chance for exposure to the right people and an opportunity to show her portfolio.

When she arrives on the call, the art director will ask to see her portfolio to review what she can do that is not shown on her composite. If she has worked at all, she will have other photos and perhaps tear-sheets, actual pages torn (hence the name "tear-sheets" although they are usually carefully cut with a razor blade) from the magazines in which they appeared. The beginning model usually won't have anything more than appears in her composite, unless she brought a few extra photos from her session with you, but the art director gets to see a little of her personality, how well she projects herself and if she comes off with a true professional image.

If the art director likes what he sees, he may say something like this: "We're going to do a shoot on Tuesday at 9:00 A.M. and I want you to come to (location) and bring (list of clothes)." If it's a fashion shoot, she won't have to bring clothes, they will be furnished, but she may have to bring a variety of shoes and several pairs of panty hose. If she's going on a shoe shoot, she won't even have to bring shoes, but she'll need four to six pairs of hose in different shades and probably several skirts. (Not all shoe shots show the skirt, so there is even leeway here.) There is a two hour minimum on jobs like these at $100 an hour plus expenses. Even if the shoot is over in fifteen minutes, the model makes $200 (less the agency's commission).

If the model has gone to an agency first and they take an interest in her, she will be told not to order composites yet because the agency wants to be involved in the selection of the photos on it. When this happens, you know the agency is definitely interested in the model. If she's told to get photography and composites before they will talk to her, they may just be trying to get rid of her, but when they are involved in the selection process, they really are interested.

The agency will give the girl a list of photographers who are known to do good work. The model must select a photographer, pay for her photographs and return with proofs from the session. The agency then looks at the photos and says, "Let's use this picture for the front and these four for the back." So, the model returns to the photographer and buys her composites. The agency up to now has invested nothing but a little time; everything else has all been up to the girl, which is the way it ought to be. The agency will not invest in her dream: if she's serious about modeling, she will take all these steps and pay for them from her own pocket.

There are times, however, when the agency person says, "I don't like this outfit or this hairstyle. They are not the way to sell you. I understand what the photographer is trying to do in these and why you chose this outfit, but it's not quite right. Why don't you do this...?" If a model gets this treatment at the agency, that's great. The agency is leading her by the hand and this is about as close as you can get to a guarantee for a successful career in modeling.

That's as much as we need to say about the composite here. There's a lot less to say about the actor's glossy, which is basically an 8 x 10 glossy print with one photograph on it, usually a large head shot; at the bottom a line negative is used to print the vital statistics of the performer. On the back of the print is photocopied the actor's resume — his formal training, workshops attended, the films he has appeared in, the stage plays performed, all the things that illustrate his acting career. Sometimes this material is not photocopied directly onto the back of the photo, but onto a sheet of paper which is then affixed to the back of the pic. If there's a lot of material, enough to take up more than one sheet, the sheets will be stapled to the photo.

Once in a great while, an actor who plans to send out hundreds of glossies in an all-out push to get his career off dead center, will have his glossies printed on a press, but this is rare. So is color, but I have seen it, usually when the actor has unusual coloring that needs to be seen for full impact.

At this time my set fee for shooting the heads for an actor's glossy is $80; that buys the performer a roll of twelve shots taken with the Hasselblad, and includes one 8 x 10 that can be taken to the nearest photo place that does quantity printing. The quantity lab is equipped to turn out the 100 or 200 prints the actor needs and do it much cheaper than a photographer can on his enlarger.

If $80 seems like inadequate pay for what the actor gets, remember that I only spend fifteen minutes

to net about $70. That works out to $280 an hour, according to the Old Math. I can live on that, can't you.

Occasionally an actor will be in a big hurry and will take the roll of film directly to the quantity lab for developing and printing there. In that case I deduct $10 because I don't have to see to the developing or make the print. I don't worry that I won't have the negs for later reorder because a head shot is a one-shot every time.

CHAPTER VI

Planning the Composite

When a beginning model calls about getting into modeling, she rarely has any idea of what clothing she should bring to the photography session. She is totally unaware of what is needed to make an effective composite, so it is up to me to direct her step by step. If we have not yet met, I ask a few questions about her height, measurements, hair color and so on. This gives me a general idea of her appearance, but I also ask other questions to determine if she's an exotic, the All-American girl next door, a tall, slender fashion model type, et cetera. As you can easily guess, it would be helpful to meet her before the session; I could much more accurately place her and the clothing she should bring.

Another thing I don't know is what she has in her closet. I don't know what her wardrobe is like or how many garments she owns. Some have such a sparse wardrobe that there's virtually nothing beyond her 501 jeans. Others have only clothing that has gone out of style, so she looks like a fugitive from the Goodwill. Her idea of a dressy outfit may be the frilly thing she wore in her sister's wedding two years ago. Don't trust her to have all the right clothes, but tell her how to get them. (More on this later).

Models rarely have any idea of how they should look or even how they want to look. When they contact me for the first time, I tell them to go through magazines and catalogs and build an idea file. I tell them to tear pictures out of the Sears or Neiman-Marcus catalog, newspapers, or magazines; "any idea you've ever seen that you think you could do as well as the model in the picture."

I want her to bring me at least twenty ideas to lay out and select from. We'll lay them out on my light table and go over them to find the best three or four

Rolls Royce, '34 Ford truck, or hansom cab, if whe wants a special vehicle, she furnishes it at her own expense.

ideas that we can use. I also warn her that if she doesn't bring a mink coat, we can't duplicate the mink coat shot, can we? Nor can we pose her in front of a Rolls Royce unless she drives up in one. And if she wants pictures with a taxi or hansom cab, she must arrange for them at the proper time and the extra expense is hers. This usually eliminates that sort of idea.

I have to create four different looks for this woman—each one distinct from the others—if she is going to have a complete and effective composite. So I ask her to bring in four totally different outfits. You must make this very clear or some models will bring four sporty outfits or four dressy ones.

First, you need an outfit that shows the figure, such as a bathing suit; another that is sporty or casual; a third that is dressy; either what she would wear to church on Sunday morning or to a bar on Saturday night; and perhaps a fourth that is high fashion. If she's less than 5'6", I don't ask for the high fashion outfit because 5'6" is the cut-off height for fashion modeling. If she's just 5'2", the only fashion look I will suggest is a petite one and then only if she's slender and carries herself well.

If she can look the part of a business person, particularly a young executive, I ask for an outfit suitable for business such as a suit or a trim skirt with white blouse and mannish jacket. But if she's definitely not the business type, I may ask for a house dress or jeans, and her husband's shirt, so we can do some shots that suggest a housewife.

A young model should come prepared to project a school girl look or the ever popular preppie style. For example, a knit shirt, a blazer, a skirt or slacks and appropriate shoes, coupled with an armful of books, says "school girl".

Whenever you go for one of these specialized looks, try to complete the picture by putting the model in a situation that complements the pose. For instance, the armful of books completes the school girl look and the business look could be augmented by having her make a presentation at a chalk board

Three different outfits, evening gown, business suit, casual garb, plus a big head are excellent choices for a good composite.

Here is one example of ways to display the figure that show life, style, and excitement. Look for other ways other than a bathing suit.

This is not a typical figure-revealing pose, nor it it a business or dress-up outfit, but it adds variety and pizzazz to her composite.

or reach into her briefcase for papers. These can still be done in front of the ubiquitous white background, however, as you are only suggesting the situation, not spelling it out in total detail.

We usually start out with the sporty or housewife looks because they are more natural for most women. If you start immediately with lingerie or swimwear, she may get the wrong idea of your intentions. It's also more natural to use a normal, not too dramatic makeup with these outfits; I prefer to start with the less heavily made up look because it's easier to add more makeup than to subtract it.

If the model is young and small— 5'2" or smaller—we can work with things that a very young girl can wear. If she's only eighteen or nineteen years old, perhaps she can easily be made to look twelve or thirteen. This is great because the more versatile she can appear, the more work she will get. The wider the age range shown on her composite, the better for her.

It is also important to change the hair styles in each of the different looks because you will be shooting head shots on each look. It is the kiss of death to have the same hairstyle in every set-up. But how do you change it if her hair is quite short? There's not much latitude in that, is there? Yes. Even hair that's cropped short can be changed in different ways. If you show the model as a housewife, sweeping while wearing jeans and a tee shirt, you can put a scarf around the hair. Add a sweat band to her tennis outfit or a hat to her fishing clothes. The use of headgear is limitless when you need to change the hair's look.

Other ploys are to wet the hair for the swim suit photos or give it a wild, wind-blown look with a fan. This works even better with long-haired girls. There should be lots of motion in the photos and blown hair looks like an outdoor location on a windy spring day. Or you can use a little goo to smooth down the hair slightly for a slick, sleek look with high fashion. Do almost the same, but not as drastic, for the business outfit.

As I said, it is important to change the hair style, at least somewhat, with each change of clothing because you're going to do head shots at each of these changes. I always do the head shots before the three-quarters or full lengths while the makeup is still perfect. Slightly marred makeup will show up in the closeups, but be invisible in the full lengths.

In the same way, when you do the bathing suit shots, you can increase believability by spritzing her with a spray bottle and show her toweling down to give the impression that she just ran out of the water. Throw a yellow tint across the background to simulate sunlight and you have July in January, which is the only way to do it in Chicago in the winter.

The clothes that are going to work best for your model are the ones that are currently featured in the fashion mags such as Vogue and Elle, or the teen magazines for the younger models. Look for clothes that are similar to those. Don't use styles that were in two years ago or the composite will be dated even before it has been printed. But how can the model who is on a limited budget afford clothes like those? Here are two ways some models use:

First, there are a number of designers in the Chicago area who will be happy to lend a dress or outfit to a model for use in a composite and her portfolio as long as the model will provide a free photograph of herself in the dress. I know many of these designers and can set it up with them to furnish clothing for my model clients. They welcome the publicity and the free photography.

The other way is less ethical, perhaps, but it may be the only answer for the women whose closet is bare of usable clothes. It is to "buy" the needed clothes from a fashionable department store with liberal return policies, then take them back when the session is finished. This may not

A casual look . . .

. . . and the perfect business outfit.

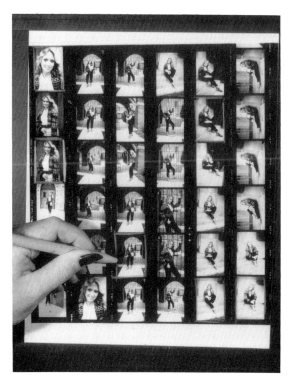

A careful selection from contact sheets is essential for effective composites.

be the most honest way to do things, but I always mention it to women who don't have the necessary clothes. If they do this, they will have the latest fashions at no expense and their composites will look great.

A third way is to borrow from a friend who has all the latest stuff and is willing to let it be worn for this quick, one-shot use. Sometimes the girl with the sparsely equipped closet has a good friend whose closet is crammed with all the newest fashions.

Don't let her wear something that is totally unsuitable for her personality, however. Aim to make her appear credible in the clothes she wears. The young girl, for instance, would be more believable in a school girl or preppie outfit than in a John Molloy "power" business suit.

If you're creating a business look, the plaid sport coat, burgundy skirt and penny loafer look doesn't cut it. IBM fires people who dress like that. You create a business look by dressing in the style that is accepted in the business community, dark suit with white shirt, tie, and suitable shoes for a man, with somewhat more flexibility for a woman. And please remember that the accessories—scarves, hats, jewelry, shoes, and props—are what everyone forgets.

You will soon find that many women will bring just one pair of shoes to go with at least three outfits. That one pair of shoes will not work with all garments because the style or color will not be right for all the looks you are creating. Lingerie requires a high heel and thin soles, a light weight appearance, perhaps with ankle straps, while a business shoe has a shorter heel, perhaps a more rounded toe, and very few of the feminine fripperies like bows or cutesy cut-outs.

If a girl wants to have something revealing in her portfolio, I'm happy to shoot it for her, but I usually speak a few words of caution to her. A teddy or baby doll pajama is not lingerie and most of them look like a loose shirt or feed sack. The garment she chooses should not reveal the nipples nor the pubic hair. It's hard to show either of these and not offend someone.

Remember that lingerie photos should give the impression that the garment is what's being sold, not the woman. The object is not to use the garment to sell sex, but to use sex to sell the lingerie and do it as subtly as possible.

If she wants a swim suit shot, she should have a good figure, just as with lingerie, but don't shoot her in one of the old-fashioned bikinis. They not only shorten the leg visually, but they lengthen the body which makes the legs seem even shorter. The type of suit is very important and the best ones are one pieces, with a very high thigh-cut. This makes the legs look like they run from the ground to the armpits and they are very flattering to most women.

Normal beach wear is worn without shoes, so your pictures would normally be done with the person bare-footed, but feet are definitely not a woman's most attractive feature. For this reason you many want to have her wear something like cork-soled sandals or you may even cut off your shot at mid-thigh and compose your picture from there on up.

If she has great legs, you can have her sit or lie so the weight is off the feet. If she stands flat-footed, she will appear somewhat foreshortened and even the greatest legs will suffer.

If the girl has the figure, Danskins are excellent for displaying it. Before you use them, decide in advance if your model has good thighs. If she does not, don't do leg shots and don't claim on her composite that she has great legs. There's enough hot air in this business without your adding any more. It is possible that you can make her legs look great in certain positions, even though she doesn't have legs that are any better than the next woman's, but if someone hires her for a leg shot, a whole day's shooting time may be lost because she won't do.

All too often models will tell lies on the comps because they think it will bring them jobs. The comp says she's 5'6" tall, but she neglects to add that she's measuring with three inch heels. Yeh, right! Don't let her put any of this garbage on her composite or it will cost her credibility and eventually she will get NO jobs because of her lying.

The model should come across as believable, so when you do lingerie, she should look somewhat sexy because of the outfit, hair and makeup. The same thing is true of high fashion: you're trying to create the sophisticated, bitchy

look that is typical of Vogue or Elle. Look at the girls in these mags and see how unapproachable they are: they look mean, don't they? There's no way the average guy could approach one of these women and talk to her because she'd cut him down *fast*. You want to get the same look for your model if she is to be believable in the role of high fashion model.

Of course, you don't want to create all of the shots with this look, just those that are high fashion. For the rest, you want to portray her as fresh, wholesome, happy or whatever other style she can project, but definitely not the same haughty look as in the fashion stuff. That's what I mean about creating a look for your client; the more looks she can show on her composite, the better chance she has of getting work as a model.

I impress on her the need to bring shoes for each outfit and all the accessories each outfit calls for; scarves, jewelry, hose, hats and props such as a furled umbrella or briefcase, essential for the business look. Even when I have told her each of these details, she always forgets something, sometimes a lot of somethings. A good idea would be to print a list of everything they might possibly need for their session; then as I speak to each model on the phone, I can check off what's needed for each look we decide on, and do it even while we speak. Then when I hang up the phone, I could slip this checklist in an envelope and mail it so she'd receive it before coming in. There would be no question about what she should bring with her; it would all be down in black and white.

These are some of the things that go into planning the composite. Because you will be working mostly with beginning models—at least, when you're a beginner yourself—planning and designing the portfolio and composite will fall principally on your shoulders and you have to be prepared to take charge of all aspects of it.

If push comes to shove, you may have to photograph her as a high fashion model if that's what it takes to fulfill her fantasies, but most of the time you will pretty much be able to control what she does and how she will look in her photographs. You do this by being knowledgeable about your trade and presenting this knowledge in a positive and forceful manner. (Please note that "forceful" does not mean overbearing or high-handed.)

After you read this book, you will know so much more about the modeling business than she does that you will be an expert by comparison. You must, however, have a good handle on it, because she will ask a lot of questions and you have to be able to answer them without any b.s. or subterfuge. Don't mislead her or screw up her understanding about modeling, or it will come home to roost. That's a lot of responsibility, so try not to be too heavy-handed in exercising control. The word is "lead" (her into doing what you perceive as right for her), not "drive."

CHAPTER VII

The Creative Team

When I got into the actual shooting part of the portfolio and composite, I found I needed people to help me, people who bring different creativities into the situation, skills that complement my own. One of those people is a makeup artist who comes to the studio and makes my clients look as good as they can for the photographs.

The makeup artist is not included in my fee but is an extra-cost option and she is paid by the model. Why don't I include her fee in mine? Because not everyone needs an artist to do her makeup and hair: an experienced model usually knows exactly how she wants to look, she knows how to spread on the goo to get precisely that look, and she may be unwilling to have anyone else fool with her face.

Other women don't want to pay the extra $40 to $50 for the artist. Most of them can be talked out of this attitude when I point out that they will spend $600 for the photographs and composites and it is false economy to try to save money by doing her own makeup. I explain that the artist will make her look so much better that her opportunities to work as a model are greatly enhanced and modeling work is what she wants, isn't it? Usually they understand and pay for the artist.

How do you find a makeup artist? One of the best ways is to visit a local salon which has five to ten women working in it and ask if there's anyone who is interested in doing makeup and hairstyling for models. Explain that there's rarely more than an hour involved and the pay is $40 for the job, but you need someone who can do a first class job of makeup and hairstyling. I explain that on the first few jobs, while she's learning what you need and want, she won't

When I am asked how much a stylist costs, I say, "She doesn't cost, she pays because she will bring out beauty you didn't know you had!"

Before . . .

get paid in cash, but will get photographs to put up in her salon. You give her a 3 x 5 of the model before makeup and an 8 x 10 of the completed makeup. (Remember to stamp your name prominently on each of the photos so you get some extra mileage out of the prints.) You will usually get one or two takers in a big salon and you start with them.

You can also find makeup stylists among the many women who sell Mary Kay or Jafra cosmetics. These are particularly good if you live in the suburbs and don't have ready access to cosmetologists skilled at working with models and photographers. Most of these salespeople are very experienced and capable of applying a first class makeup, but try to find one who can style the hair, too. There are not so many of these, but keep hunting and you'll locate the ideal person who is willing to be at your beck and call. (Check the laws regarding the hair and makeup business in your state; some states have tougher laws for cosmetologists than for brain surgeons, and you may not be able to use Mary Kay people unless they are licensed.)

For the woman who can't or won't pay the stylist, there is one more source of good makeup—a nearby Merle Norman store. For those of you who don't recognize that name, Merle Norman is a cosmetic franchise that uses a complete makeup as its main sales tool. Women sit on a stool in the store and get a complete make-over by the operator. Merle Norman sales people are well trained and do an excellent job, very subtle and never too heavy, and there is no charge for this. They know—based on sales figures—that for every makeup they do, they will sell a certain dollar amount. They also know that they will not sell every woman who comes to them and that some women are coming in just because they have a big date that night and want to look their best. It's all part of the job and the law of averages is their best ally.

But, because the Merle Norman makeup is usually applied quite subtly, your model should ask for a heavier job, one that won't wash out under fairly flat lighting. Then you (or she) must be prepared to add any additional accents your first Polaroid exposure indicates.

Once you are established in the model photography business, artists and stylists will come to you looking for work. I get two or three calls every week from people

. . . during . . .

. . . and after.

wanting to do my makeup jobs, most of them freelancers working out of a salon or their homes. Obviously, they want to make money for their services, but my advice is to test them, several times, and pay in free prints before adding them to your list of approved people. Some are good and some are not and some will waste your time. One man who came in for a try-out was a expert at makeup, the very best, but he was so slow I never asked him back: he took two hours, the job was excellent—truly flawless—but two hours? No way!

You build a creative team based on your past experiences with each individual. But while you're starting out, you can get burned if you don't discover a makeup is bad until the film is developed. How can you prevent this awkward situation? Polaroid is what keeps you from a re-shoot when the makeup is bad. I take a tight Polaroid of the head when the artist is finished, and I inspect it very carefully to see if the area around the eyes is too white or dark or if something else is wrong. Maybe the makeup is fluorescing blue when the flash goes off, or it just may not look right to me. If any of these things happens, I go over the Polaroid with the artist and we decide what has to be done to make it work. If it doesn't look right on the Polaroid, I know it won't look good on any other film, so it has to be done over until the Polaroid looks okay.

Incidentally, if you get an artist who fights you about redoing a makeup that

looks bad on the Polaroid, drop him or her. You want to build a team that works well together, not a bunch of prima donnas who stamp their dainty little feet and insist they know what you want better than you do. Life is too short for that nonsense and besides the world is full of pleasant, easy to get along with people who would be delighted to work with you.

Polaroids are the best way to teach a makeup artist what's wrong and how to do it right for model's photos. I don't always know how to correct the glitch, but I know when it's wrong and I can tell them when it should be "softer" or "harder."

I say, "It should not look like this. The effect I want is so and so. I should not be able to see a streak there, so tone it down. I don't want to see the eyes isolated in pools of white; you have to eliminate that."

So the artist goes to work again with the Polaroid stuck on the mirror in front of her and she works until another Polaroid shows me that it's right. Does this bother the cosmetologist? It better not if she wants me to recommend her to my models. Does it bother the model? Not at all, she knows that all this is being done to make her look

Do you begin to see how much the stylist can add to your success? The marvelous part is that the client pays for her expertise.

sensational, so she doesn't care about the extra time it takes.

I use the Polaroid back that fits my Hasselblad for these test shots, but if you do not have a camera that readily accepts instant film, buy a Polaroid camera, an adjustable one that will let you come close enough to your subject to get a big head. The adjustable ones are the discontinued 180 or 195 or the Konica Instant Press. This is the next best thing to the Polaroid back and it can also be used to take family snaps by your non-photographer spouse.

Basically, the makeup artist/hair stylist is the only person you will need on your immediate creative team, but there are other people who can be considered as part of it when you get into bigger jobs.

If you get involved with a project such as the dance wear catalog we are now doing, your creative team will grow to include several makeup people, perhaps a separate hair stylist, an assistant cameraman, and a lot of separate subcontractors such as the person who designs the catalog, the one who separates the transparencies, and the printer. When the job is done, each of the people involved in the project can take credit for it by pointing to the catalog and saying, "I did the makeup for these girls," "I did the separations," or "I did this superb photography."

The photography on this job really *was* superb. How do I know? The client said so: "This photography is superb, the best we have had in twenty-six years. In more than a quarter century, you are the first photographer ever to do this catalog three years in a row, and that's precisely because you gave us superb photography."

The reason he had gotten poor photography in the past is that he was not willing to pay for a first class photographer. Prior to my landing the job, the most he had paid for photography was $500 a day when the going rate for a quality, down-town Chicago photographer is $2000. I didn't get $2000 for this job either, in fact I got only a little more than half my usual day rate, but the job lasts two months, so I do very well on it. Besides, I raised the price the second year and I'll keep raising it every year that I have the job.

And because they also spent more for better color separation and printing, their catalog is an excellent sales piece for their line and an outstanding one for me. I know it will bring in new work for this studio for several years because it is so outstanding.

So the concept of a creative team is an important one. In the beginning, it may consist of just you and your wife (and only if she is really competent at applying makeup), but if you do your part, it will grow, so be sure to get the best people you can. Incidentally, a part of your creative team should be people you can brainstorm with, preferably other photographers with whom you can sit and share your problems and lay out your thoughts for evaluation.

I know one group of portrait photographers who meet every year for a long weekend during which each person lays out his plans and advertising and promotions for the coming year so each of the others can criticize or suggest improvements. Every person benefits from the thinking of the others and each one goes away much richer than he came.

If you and I trade dollars, neither of us makes anything, but if we trade ideas, we are richer because of it. (Incidentally, none of these studio owners are in direct competition with each other.)

The firecracker hairdo and the glittery upsweep . . . these are all things that a good stylist can do.

I am often asked how long the cosmetologist stays after she does the initial makeup. She may stay only until I am satisfied with the Polaroid check print, or she may stay while we set up for the second "look." We are going to do four looks during the normal session and I like the artist to stay long enough to do the second one. She has been hired for one hour and it's not hard to get to the second look in that space of time, so she does a second hair-do and touches up the makeup before leaving.

It is important to change the hair for each of the four looks you are planning to do, partly to create a wide age range in her various looks. An even more important reason is to make each hair-do suit the outfit she wears in the photos. Let me draw you a picture: the model arrives and you see that she is very much a part of the current scene, so you arrange her hair in one of the popular styles and shoot a roll of her in typical punk clothing.

Then you dress her as a business executive in a suit and horned rim glasses, but you leave her hair up in a modified Mohawk. Is her hair in character for the outfit? Of course not. In fact, you should always vary the hair from look to look. Remember that you're going to do big heads with each change of clothing and each set-up should look as different from the other as possible. A different hair style with each change is important. Do a sleek style for the business or high fashion look and a much softer style for the teenage or preppie image. Don't ever leave her hair the same from look to look. The agency won't like it and neither will people who might hire her. It could be the kiss of death for her new career.

The hair *must* be changed even if it's very short. In some shots you can try for the wet look or use a fan to get a wind-blown impression. This works even better with long hair which swishes nicely in the breeze of the fan. Always try for the look of action and motion in the photos, even if it's just making the hair blow or move with the swinging of the head. It is this action-motion look that will distinguish your pictures from those of the amateurs and make your services very much in demand.

Normally we start with a lighter makeup, then go to a more sophisticated look which usually calls for heavier makeup. This gives the makeup artist the opportunity to create two distinct looks in the one hour. The high fashion look, for instance, would be done after a housewife look because fashion requires a heavier makeup.

I don't try to change the whole look for each change of clothing, but I try to put some change into everything. If the model arrives wearing jeans or looks a bit punkish, we might start out with a wild hair-do that's appropriate to what a kid would wear today. That's the young style and it's often seen in the magazines that are on the stands right now.

From there we would tone it down to a more conservative look and at each step we would refine the hair-do and add more makeup. Minor differences are added or subtracted—hats, hairbands or props that create a different look. If the stylist leaves after the second makeup, I depend on the model to change her hair to suit the change in garments. Of course, there are seldom any radical changes to be made at this time, just the subtle refinements any woman can do to her own hair and face.

These minor changes and refinements are very necessary, however. If the model has the same hair with several outfits, one of those looks can't be used because of the static hairstyle. You must have change of hair with each change of outfit, even if it's only pulling the hair back or putting on a sweat band. If you don't change the hair, it's like paper dolls where you only change the clothes. The agency wants to see variety not only in clothes, but in the entire

The first photo is without makeup or professional styling. The second is light makeup and hair suitable for casual or business wear. The third look is a full evening makeup and hair to match.

look. Variety means versatility to the agency, and it's a lot easier to sell a versatile person than one who has only a single look.

I am often asked if a photographer needs a representative, or "rep" as they are more often called. (A rep is not normally a part of your *creative* team, but may be necessary to your *overall* team, so let's discuss him/her here.) If you're going to specialize in model's photography, the answer is no, you don't need a rep and no rep would work for you because the job would pay only peanuts. If you want to go after commercial and illustrative work, however, a rep can be useful, maybe even valuable.

Let's take a moment to discuss the function of a rep and how he or she works and is paid. The rep's function is to drum up business for me, business that I can't get myself for one reason or another. It is sales work of a very high and intense order.

Let's assume that I don't do as much business as I would like with the J. Walter Thompson advertising agency, so my rep begins to call on various art directors there. Let's also say that she talks to a certain art director and learns that he is dissatisfied with the photographer working on one of his accounts. She also knows that I can do that type of work almost better than anything else I do. So she pushes for the account and lands it for us.

The rep is paid twenty-five per cent of the job she brings into the studio from that art director. Not only that, *she also gets twenty-five percent of any other business that comes in from that A.D. in the future whether or not she actively promoted that subsequent business*. Does she deserve it? I think so because my rep can say and do things for me that I can't do for myself, such as, "Art Ketchum is the greatest photographer west of Art Kane." I can't do that if I want to be taken seriously. She gets away with it because she knows most of the photographers in Chicago and knows what I can and can't do compared to them, so she is very believable. Even more important, she can ask for and get more money (sometimes a lot more) for my services that I can, usually enough more to pay her commission and show additional profits for me.

So a rep can be very valuable. I've gotten work from reps when I have had them in the past, but it has usually involved a hassle. It's hard to find a *good* rep and it took up too much of my time. In the end I decided that a rep was not for me, but you may want to try it for yourself, so here's my best advice.

Don't hire a rep on a salary or draw or there will be money going out for perhaps six to twelve months with none coming in. If you're rich, that may be okay, but an outside salesperson—which is what your rep is—cannot be supervised the way other studio employees can be. More than once I have called a rep at home at 11:00 A.M. and heard her answer the phone, none of them had a good excuse for goofing off. So, if you hire a rep, put him or her on commission only, no salary or draw. To make any money, the rep must make sales, which is why you hired her in the first place.

When you pay only commissions, you don't have to support this person, so you can pay an even higher commission than twenty-five percent, maybe thirty or thirty-five. Just be sure your rep knows how much to charge for your services so you don't lose anything.

CHAPTER VIII

Posing the Model

I started to begin this chapter by saying that posing the model is the easiest part of the job, but I caught myself in time. It is true that the posing part of the job is not too tough when you are fully trained and experienced, but for the beginner at photographing models, it may seem overwhelming.

It is not that difficult, however, if you take it step by step. When the model is dressed in her first outfit and the makeup is complete, take your test Polaroid, (a close-up of the face), to check the makeup for anything that's not visible to the naked eye, but will show up on color film. When you take the shot, you have already set up the lights for the first pose and your camera is in approximate position.

What next? If everything looks good, start taking photographs. I usually take the big heads first, then progress to head and shoulders, and then three-quarters and full length shots. This progression is a natural way to do things and the best part of it is that you do the easier shots—the close-ups—first, then the tougher shots afterwards. If you are like most of us, the tight shots are easy, but arranging the full lengths into pleasing patterns calls for much more ability. There's so much more flesh to deal with and it takes time to learn how to pose full lengths and three-quarter poses that look good and show off the model to her best advantage.

There are exceptions to this general approach to taking the photos, but it generally follows this pattern: with each outfit I do the close-ups, then gradually pull back to the full length poses. I may occasionally see a head shot that looks so good I immediately go to a full length while she holds a facial expression or

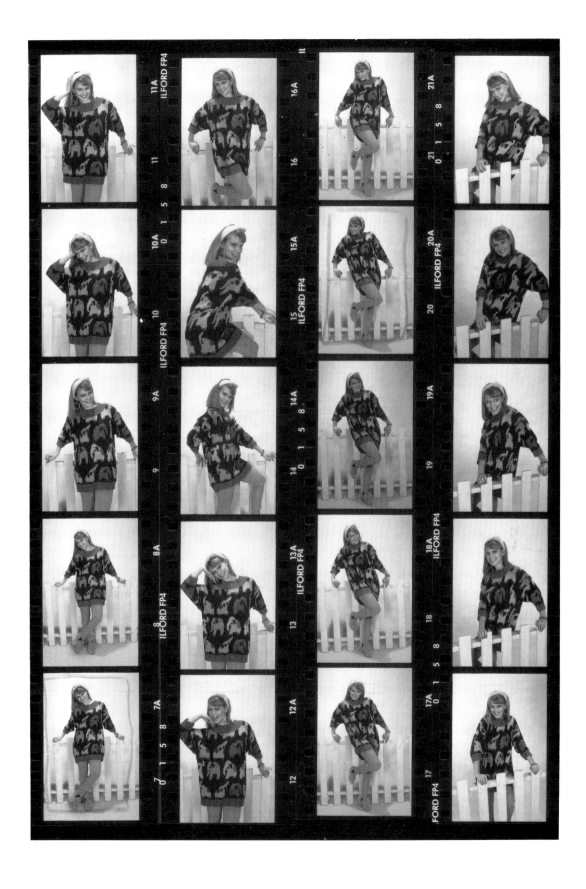

turn of the head, but this is not the norm. (We are printing some entire proof sheets here so you can see this movement from close-ups to full length poses just as it happens in actual practice.)

After I do a roll on one look, the client changes into her next set of garments and we repeat the process—big heads, head and shoulders, three-quarters and full lengths, until we have done the four outfits. At that point I should have a good selection of poses for her to choose from, including several good big heads for the front of the composite.

There will always be exceptions to this rule for those women who follow your suggestion and bring in a number of tear sheets from magazines and catalogs with poses they want to duplicate. This is not a big problem, however, you have to keep everything in mental sequence. If she shows you a photo of a woman in an evening gown and asks for a similar pose, you have to remember to take it at the proper moment.

Don't do as I did on one occasion. I forgot to take a particular shot the woman wanted very much, and she didn't remember it either, until she was in the elevator leaving the building. She came charging back because that shot was important to her portfolio. She changed back into the proper dress and we did another ten shots until I was satisfied we had what we needed. It cost a few

minutes and extra film and proofing to get what the customer wanted, but if I had been alert, there would have been no extra cost and I would have got the shot at the proper time.

I know many of you are looking to this chapter to find out how to set up Pose #2AA, but you will find very little of that type of information here. If you are to be a success in model photography, by all means avoid the stereotyped freeze poses taught at the modeling schools. Learn how to get flowing poses that are full of life and action. These are the (non) poses the agencies are looking for.

Here are some ways to get them: 1) Use an electric fan on a stand as a mini wind machine to blow garments and hair in shots depicting action. The fan doesn't have to be too strong to give the effect of quite a breeze, especially when you have the model lean into the breeze as though bucking a heavy wind. Let her dramatize it. Action is what you want to simulate.

2) Have the model move. Ask her to dance, not all over your set, but

Jaleigh

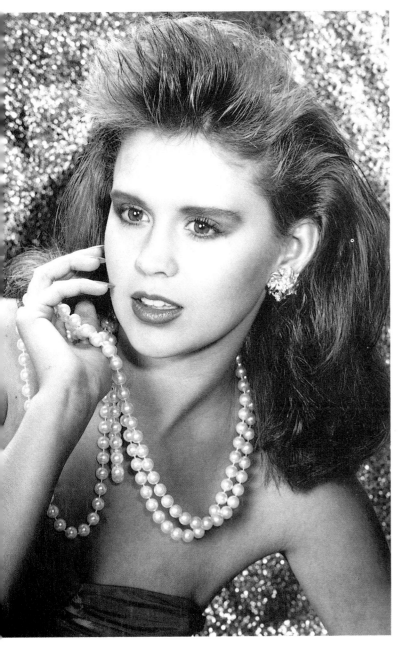

right in place so her movements provide the action you need. Don't let her boogie too far from the place where you position her or she'll get off the background or move out of focus.

3) Have her touch and lean against things like fence posts or ladders or high backed chairs. When enough weight is supported on these things, she can lean into the line of the photograph and produce action just by being well placed within the frame.

4) A favorite ploy of mine is to get several magazine pictures that show related poses and have the model move from pose to pose as I try to capture the essence of what she is doing. That sounds hard, but in practice, it is much easier than it sounds. You may find it easier to walk through the poses several times so the model gets the feel of the movements before you pick up your camera. Once she has the rhythm mastered, take your shots.

What you want to capture in your photographs is a feeling of movement as she flows from one pose to another. "Flow" is a word that is bandied about widely in this business. Grasp the idea of movement in your photographs and agents will say, "I really like the flow of your work." Fail to grasp it and they will say, "There's something wrong with the flow of these pictures." So pay close attention to Uncle Art, who has worked with models closely for nearly ten years.

Don't handle the merchandise, which is another way of saying, "Don't touch the models." They don't know you and they are half expecting you to come on to them, so don't touch! Learn how to direct the model into position with your voice, some body English, plus a little posing yourself.

I will come back to the voice part in a moment, but body English simply means that just as you use the position of your body and its movements to tell a pin-ball machine or a bowling ball what to do, so too, you can use your own bodily contortions to direct a model into the position you want her to take. This is easier to show than to tell, but I'm sure most of you have done just what I have described and you know that it works.

The third item above is what I call "mirroring the pose." It just means that when you want her to strike a pose, you can tell her how to do it more easily if

you will assume the same pose, but in reverse, like a mirror image. Tell her this right at the beginning and you will have no problems making yourself clear. Just say, "I'm going to show you some of these poses by posing myself. As you look at me you don't have to figure out which way I want you to pose because I'll take a mirror pose for you. That means that I'll use my right hand if I want you to use your left hand or I'll turn to the left if I want you to turn to the right. Okay?" Then I run through it a time or two with her until I'm sure she understands.

But the tool I use most in posing her is my voice. When this book was in the planning stages, my editor was at a shooting session with me and he recorded my chatter as I worked with the model. What he got was very typical of what I say when I'm working. Here's a sample:

"...Now put your hand up on the railing. Maybe not. Come forward a couple of feet. Like this. Yea. Beautiful." (click)

"This time I want to go for something dramatic, arms out, looking down and we're going real high fashion. That's good, that's good." (click)

"A little too much bend at the waist, I'm getting lines there. Pull it down tighter at the waist. There you go. Yes, that's good." (click)

"Okay, now give me a little bit of a body turn, turn one foot out. I don't like the feet position. Yes, that's it, that's it. (click) Excellent, good, good." (click)

"A little more pizzazz on the arm that's turned out. That's it. Good. Great. (click) That looks fantastic." (click)

"Okay, we'll see what this looks like and kinda run through it. Run through it, turn. Yeah, that's nice." (click)

"Let the arm go out a little more. That's it. (click) Give me a little turn and a little bend in the elbow, a little more, more. (click) Now a little more bend in the elbow, and you're coming around, that's nice. (click) Very nice."

"Look off more distant, beyond me, that's it, that's it, but a little too much to the side. Don't let the eyes go too much to the side, keep them pointed right down the bridge of the nose. Keep them more centered in the socket, otherwise I see too much white. Turn the head when you turn the eyes. That's it, good." (click)

"Now turn the eyes a little bit so you're looking off into the distance, the same direction your head is pointed. Very nice, yeah, good, I like it." (click)

"Now go back and touch the wood on the background. Okay, excellent, excellent. (click) Now touch both hands to it as if you are leaning back on it, but don't lean back on it or it will fall, but put your backside to it and your back flat against it. Put a hand up on the railing, the other hand, higher up on the railing. Yes, that's it, good, excellent. (click) That's what I'm looking for right there. All right, very nice." (click) (click)

"Give me a turnaround so you're almost facing the background, putting the hands up there kinda high and start looking back toward me just a little. That's a better head shot. (click) Switch over and do some, let's see where I'm at, that's good. Touch the railing and look this way, good, keep going around, head all around, that's nice." (click)

Now, looking this way towards the camera. Beautiful, okay, excellent, excellent. (click) Exactly what I'm looking for, that's nice with the hands on the railing. I'm really going for the face here more than anything. Come a little more, oh, that's it." (click)

"This is somewhat the same thing we did a minute ago. Good, let that arm go out and get a little more flair in that arm, the right one. Let that go out, give me...we're looking for a real...no, the other one, put more bend in it. Yea, that's it, but I'm looking for a dramatic feel, little more bend in it. Pull the tummy in as tight as you can, there you go. Great, great." (click)

"Excellent, now let that other arm go out almost like you're catching your

balance. Beautiful. (click) Okay, one more time. Lift that back foot almost like you're taking a step, heel off the ground. Tighten the tummy. That's great. Excellent. (click) Nice look. Looking off into the distance again. Good, good. (click) We got it."

A lot of chatter, but it communicates and causes her to move, move, move so the photos are filled with action and sometimes a bit of tension. There's a dynamic in the posing that you don't get if your comments are limited to "turn here, turn there, smile." Just note that I never shut up, I never stop talking. This is vital with new models who are scared and need a lot of reassurance.

When I'm talking, it keeps her relaxed and comfortable because someone who knows what he is doing has taken charge and she doesn't have to worry about who's running things. A strong take-charge guy has taken charge and will make it all come out right.

That's what all this chatter accomplishes.

The minute you stop talking, she's under the microscope. The lights are on and the camera is focused on her and she's standing all alone in the middle of the white paper background. And, and, and. Watch the tension build. I keep talking so there's no time for her to think.

Also, I continually tell her how well she's doing and how beautiful that pose is, and how lovely she is. ("Are you sure you've never modeled before? My! You move so gracefully, like you've been doing it all your life. You have a lot of natural ability.") Am I lying to her? Well, maybe a little at the beginning, but as she gains confidence from listening to me say she's doing great, she really does begin to move more like a pro, to show that she has what it takes to succeed as a model.

I kinda fall in love with all my models, whether they're male or female, child or crone, I fall in love with them at least a little and for at least a time. And when you love someone, you strive to find nice things to say about her, don't you? So I look for a feature that's very attractive, and I always find one. Hair, eyes, gracefulness, whatever, and I comment on it whenever I get the chance: "You really have great legs, so let's be sure we feature them so you look great on your composite." Or, "You have a super personality; let's see how we can make that come through in as many of these photos as we can."

I find something that's beautiful about the person and I work to bring it out in her photos and I let her know what I'm doing ("I just gotta get some good shots of that fantastic profile!") and pretty soon she relaxes and is quite comfortable. No longer does she feel like she's in the dentist's office, but with a friend who really likes her and says so. We all enjoy that and we eat it up. I do, how about you?

There's a little danger in doing this. You don't ever want the model to think you are coming on to her, even if you'd like to. Keep all your remarks about her beauty on the impersonal level as much as you can, so she is not offended. I have an advantage over some of you in this matter as I have grown daughters and I'm plainly old enough to be the father of many of these girls. If you're

young and a nice guy, you may find the girls reacting seriously to your chatter. Keep it impersonal so this doesn't happen.

The photographer who is unable to talk and keep it flowing, will have much less success than the one who can. So, practice on your spouse or other friends until it becomes second nature to keep the talk going as you work. It's like the so-called stream of consciousness school of writing, wherein the writer just starts with a thought and goes to the thought that spins off the first one and so keeps a whole book going from the recesses of his mind. But this stream wins friends for you and makes a lot of money, too.

I admit to being one of the quiet ones in the beginning, but I learned to talk when I saw the difference it makes in the model, so it's something you can learn. Now I never seem to run out of words as I try to spark life and emotion in the model. If I can get the reactions I want and get them on film, I am a success and I will make a lot of money doing something that's really not hard work.

What I have to be sure of is that the model never has time to talk and never has to ask, "What do you mean?" even if I direct her to turn by saying, "Turn anything you want to turn and if it's not right, I won't take it and if it's good, I will." That's about as loose a set of instructions as I can give her, but sometimes it produces perfect pictures.

If I don't think a model looks good in a shot, I won't take it. I know some photographers who will shoot anything they have set-up, even if it looks bad. They don't want to seem indecisive to the model, but I don't hesitate to abort a shot if it's not right. Is it be-cause I'm more secure and sure of my identity, as one person said? I don't know, but I don't think I make my model unsure if I admit that I have set up a sec-ond rate pose.

You can learn what are ac-ceptable poses by scanning all the fashion magazines and cata-logs. Notice how many of them feature movement and motion as an integral part of the picture. Don't deliberately set out to copy these photos, except at the very beginning, but look for the feeling and emotion in them and strive to evoke the same emo-tions in your photographs. Keep at it until you know you have gone from an amateur photogra-pher of models to a professional, then you are ready to begin your business.

CHAPTER IX

Backgrounds, Locations & Props

The ideal basic background for photographers working with models is a white one that is as high as your ceiling and at least ten feet wide, although wider is better. It should be coved where it meets the floor so that it blends into the floor, which should also be white. "Coved" means that where the wall meets the floor it gradually bends until it is level with the floor. This gradual bend makes the line where the wall meets the floor invisible rather than an abrupt slash cutting across the lower part of the picture.

The same thing can be done with a roll of white background paper. Hang the roll as high as you can, then pull it down like a window blind until you have about eight or ten feet of it lying on the floor. That gives you a white area for the model to stand on as well as the white ground behind the model and it curves at the floor line so you get the same effect as the covered wall, except it is more fragile and susceptible to dirt and rips. It is also a little narrower (only nine feet wide) than the wall I suggested and this forces you to stay alert to the movement of the model.

When you pose your model in front of the background (correctly lighted), the final image will stand out from the background and be isolated from it. It is a traditional way to present a person or product when you want all attention concentrated on her or it. There are, of course, other ways to back up your model, but this is one of the best for portfolio work where you want to feature the model with great emphasis.

The correct way to light this background to render it a pure white on your prints, is to flood it evenly with light that meters stronger than the subject lighting. For instance, if your correctly lighted model meters at f:8, the light at the background should read stronger than that, perhaps f:11. It's a good idea to test this with a Polaroid when you begin to experiment with your basic lighting.

The best way to get this even light on the background is to place two lights on either side of it, aiming them so they overlap in the middle. The lights should be placed well to the sides so they are out of the picture and they should be close enough to the background so none of their light falls on the subject. Some photographers add a light coming from above, but this is not really necessary.

When you meter a subject in front of the white background, use an incident, not a reflected meter. All that light bouncing off the white surface will influence the reading of a reflected meter, so stick with the incident model.

There are several grey background papers that are useful. Dove Grey is much lighter than an 18% grey card and it can be used just like the white paper if you put plenty of light on it, perhaps another stop. It can also be underlighted to add a little tone behind the model.

I find Thunder Grey very useful because of the effects I get when I use it with colored gels. For instance, if I cover one of my background lights with a blue gel and the other with red gel, where they overlap there will be tone of purple. The shade of purple depends on the amount of light striking that area. If none of the light on the subject falls there and the background light is balanced with the light on your model, it will be a quite deep purple. If the background lights are quite strong in relation to the subject lighting, the background will go more toward violet. The same thing happens if the foreground lights spill into the purple area and dilute the color. Which effect is better? Hey, there's no "better" in this business: it's what looks good and works with the subject.

If I use a medium blue background and throw a light with a pink gel at the center of it, the background is blue with a pink spot in its center and all around the edges of the pink spot the pink and blue begin to blend together. Where this happens there is life and vibrancy and all sorts of

White is the ideal basic background for studio photography.

pretty colors in between. It's a very pretty effect that you can't get in any other way.

Most of us are limited in the number of lights we have and the amount of power we can push through them, so it's not always possible to have as many lights as our imagination dictates. However, most of the special things I speak of here can be duplicated quite easily with just three lights. Put the main light

With various background papers and the proper lighting, you can produce any effect you desire.

in a soft box or bounce it from an umbrella. This is the main light on the subject; it is balanced with a fill board (explained under "Lighting"), while the background is illuminated by the other two lights. If you get these two lights, you can have a very wide range of effects at virtually no cost.

It's easy to get very powerful and different effects by using colored backgrounds and lighting them with colored gels. If, for instance, you put up a blue paper and get one of your background lights with yellow — Wow! Look at the green spot you get on the background.

Certain colors seem to work better than others with different complexions. You'll have to experiment with this, as it is a very subjective reaction. You'll also find that what works great with pale white skin may fall totally apart with latino or black skin. But this is something only you can decide, so test, try, experiment before doing a "for real" sitting. Have it down cold when that first paying model comes in and you'll never have to fumble.

Don't attempt to use any sort of painted backdrop, especially the kind that are favored by portrait photographers. They simply won't work with this kind of photography and will instantly classify you as a portraitist with the agencies and that's just what they don't want.

Stick to solids for all indoor backgrounds. If you need a background that's not a solid color, use your lights to cast shadows on it. Or pull down a darker background and throw a spot in the middle of it. Use light creatively with darker backgrounds and you will surprise even yourself with what you can do.

Background paper by itself seems dead and lifeless to me, even when it is

The simplest lighting and background . . .

lighted separately from the subject. Perhaps it's the flat finish of the paper, but when colored light is spritzed on it, it comes alive. Gloss surfaces seem to have depth and shine and richness which flat ones don't, but the mixing of the colors changes all that and the flat surface is much more lively. It's not necessary to use a contrasting color gel on the light, a darker blue on light blue seamless will still make the color pop. It also intensifies the color and increases separation.

The portrait photographer who paints his background makes it light in the center and increasingly darker toward the edges. The effect of this is to brighten the middle of the background just as I do with a light. They "fake" a light in the center of the background.

Another thing I do to jazz up the background for head shots is to buy remnants of fabric at sewing stores for fifty cents or a dollar. I tack one on the background and position the head right in front of it for a dynamite look. I may light it from a sharp angle to pick up the wrinkles for a sculptured texture. Recently I found I can do the same thing with a piece of roll background by crumpling it, then smoothing it out again. The result with a very acute lighting angle is the look of facets in the paper, like diamonds or crystal.

. . . can produce dynamite results.

For an even more striking effect, add a frontal light with a color gel to the set-up. Now the previously shadowed areas are filled with color, while the previously lighted areas are probably burned out and showing up as white areas.

It's only my opinion, but I think backgrounds can be the single biggest thing you can do to lift your model's photography above the others and it's important to light them just as well as you light the subject. Proper lighting will give a dimensional quality to your background that you get in no other way. The easy way to have your backgrounds right on the money is to shoot a Polaroid as soon as you think everything's

The liberal use of Polaroid test shots brings peace of mind. Since I started to use Polaroid, I sleep well and my stomach never churns a bit.

ready. That's the proof of the pudding and it's especially important in the beginning; later on, experience will put you very close to the mark even when you forget your meter.

If you use umbrellas to light your subjects, you have a lot of control over the effects you can get with them by feathering the light or sliding the lamp head up and down on the shaft. You can let a little, a lot, or no light at all spill over onto the background. You can have a hard or soft light on the subject at the same time you do these other things. You are limited only by your ingenuity.

When you hang the background, let it sweep forward just like a paper background so the model stands on it and you will have a background that's uniquely yours, yet you can change it between every sitting, if you choose, with just a little more paint. I am not suggesting that you make a background just like the portrait backgrounds you can buy, just that you experiment to get a different look in some of your photographs.

Here's another way to make an interesting background: get a large canvas drop cloth from a paint store and splash it with various colors of latex paint. Or you can use spray cans and their intense colors will make a more graphic effect, but the background will still be seen as cloth. Don't worry about the seams or the wrinkles that will show when you hang it behind your model. They add to the effect.

The drop cloth I bought was a too hot, too much bright white, so I took it and a packet of Rit to the laundromat and dyed it blue. That was much prettier, but I wasn't through yet. I created a cloudlike shape on it with a spray can, not a real cloud look, just a vague resemblance, then I dabbed and splattered some more.

Have you seen the photographs Irving Penn makes when he records primitive people in Africa or New Guinea? He does them by natural light in a tent he sets up and he uses a grungy looking drop cloth for a background.

Outdoor locations . . .

. . . can take may forms.

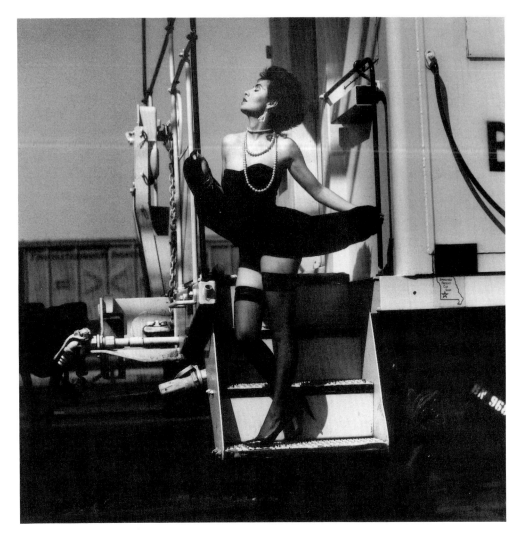

Is the incongruity of a railroad car and lovely legs too much for you or do you find it as exciting as I do?

That was the effect I wanted to achieve, a totally different feel than the same old boring seamless.

When it comes to outdoor or location photography, I am cramped somewhat by having a studio in an area of Chicago that has already been prepared for rehabilitation. What I'm saying is that most of the demolition work has been completed and for blocks this area resembles Hiroshima on the day after. That may be great if you're doing photos to illustrate World War II, but for a model's portfolio, it limits the photographs you can take.

Within a ten minute drive, however, is a museum with magnificent steps, a good bit of the downtown area and Lincoln Park and the Zoo. These are all summer locations and I try to avoid the outdoors in the winter. Chicago winters are fiercely cold and I avoid location shooting during the winter months, not just because neither my cameras nor I function well in that cold, but because in the winter the lighting is a blah grey most of the time. There are no cast

Sunlight through a window can provide an effective "location" shot.

shadows and the leaves are gone from the trees. Chicago snow is never pretty; within ten minutes it is mud colored.

For these and other reasons, I work inside in the winter. One apparent exception is that I can work in the hallway of my building (still under reconstruction) and get shots that *appear* to have been taken outdoors. Sunlight streams through a window onto a plastered wall that looks just like a stuccoed exterior. It's an effective "location" shot.

In the other seasons I do outside photography. I try to mix in one or two shots that are plainly done outdoors because this upgrades the appearance of the composite, makes it look more exciting and promotes the girl as being more experienced than she actually is.

When we go to a location that is some distance away, I charge extra for it. If the model says she has a horse and wants pictures taken with it, but the horse is in Barrington, (an hour away), I say I'll be glad to do it, but I'll have to charge

Props add life to a photograph and quite often can suggest the next pose in a session.

extra for it, probably $35. That won't come close to covering the extra time, but I like to do this sort of picture; it makes a better portfolio and it is also enjoyable. The $35 is just to cover some of my expenses.

When something like this happens, I will usually make these horse photos the last of the session and I plan some extra time while I'm in Barrington so I can shoot a few pictures for my stock file. This is just for my own fun and to build my file photos.

If I told the model that I'd have to charge her what it's worth — probably $200 — she would never pay it. I figure, however, that she won't balk at the $35, so part of my expenses are covered. If even that sum is too much for her, it isn't worth it to me to spend an hour or more away from the studio.

Some exotic locations just happen. For instance, it would normally be quite expensive to take models aboard a boat and do pictures there, but I have a friend whose deluxe cruiser is mine for the asking because he's excited about having young, pretty models aboard to be photographed. There seems to be

nothing sexual in this, he just likes pretty girls and having them aboard, so he goes out of his way to make them feel at home and comfortable. He is so outgoing with them that occasionally one of them gets the wrong idea and comes on to this older man, but he frankly tells them he isn't after their bodies, he just wants them to have fun. I have paid him by giving him prints of the girls aboard the vessel and with a very nice portrait of his boat.

It's a good idea to search out locations in the immediate area of your studio before you need them. When you go looking for locations, there are two general types to look for, those that just furnish a nondescript background for your models and those that can be integrated into the picture to jazz it up. Good examples of the first type are a blank wall, easily blended foliage or a rise where you can silhouette the model against the sky.

For the second type, look for modern sculp-

"Pearls" and other assorted items from the prop closet.

ture (every large city has it as part of the public landscape) or striking modern buildings. Sometimes flower beds or flowering trees can be made an actual part of the photograph by placing the model in the middle of them, rather than using them as out-of-focus color blobs in the background.

As for props, you want to have on hand those things that can be added to your photographs to generate the feeling of a pose. You do not want to set up an entire office when you photograph a woman in a business suit, but adding a briefcase, a sheaf of 8 1/2 x 11 papers or a telephone gives a little touch of truth that somehow makes the photo appear real.

So gradually gather together a supply of props to keep handy in your camera room. Having them at hand makes it easy to get the type of pictures the agencies want because they add variety to the composite. And quite often the possession of a prop will suggest the next pose and make it easy to go from one set-up to the next. Props can come from anywhere—something you're about to discard at home may be a perfect prop. The Goodwill Stores are full of things you can use and Pier One Imports sells dozens of neat and useful items for a dollar or two. Almost anything is good for your prop closet, so make it a habit never to throw away anything without first evaluating it for use as a prop. As you look through this book, see how many of my props could have come from discards.

An excellent prop for most portfolios is one or more other people. If a lifeless prop can add reality to your photos, think of what other people can do. By putting another person in the frame, you generate an interaction between them that can add unknown dynamics to a portfolio. This is especially valuable when you are working on location, but it's also a good idea when you are doing full lengths on a white background. There is so much white to be broken up and sometimes you just can't do it successfully. The extra person helps block out part of the whiteness and adds another shape in the frame.

When you add another person, it's a good idea in most cases to subdue that one either by softening the focus, by placing him/her in a subordinate position or by darkening. Don't forget that you want to feature the model (she's the one paying you to make her photos), so the other person must be kept in the background in one way or another.

The first way to subordinate the second person is to position him behind the model relative to the camera. The person nearest to the camera automatically assumes the dominant position in a photograph, all other things being equal. In addition, in all indoor photographs the person nearest the camera is usually lighted more strongly than the one further away, which adds to the dominance of the front person.

That leads us to the second way to make the model more important than the "prop" person; you light the prop less brightly than the model. If the second person is a stop or two darker than the model, he/she is effectively made less important than the model. This is quite easy to do if you keep the prop person

further from the lights and the camera than the model. This is a mental trick. Our minds tell us the less brightly lighted person is not as important.

The final way is by selective focus. Make the model sharp and the prop person soft. Again, when you do this, the mind says that the fuzzy one is not as important as the sharp one.

It's easy to use all three of these effects in your photographs if you keep the second person in the background. Because the prop person is farther away from the lights, he is less brightly lighted than the model and probably a little less sharp than she is. So the mere act of placing the #2 person further from the camera automatically brings into action the other two rules for rendering him less important than your model.

Learn how to use your backgrounds, locations and props to accentuate the positive things about your models and you will at once begin to improve your work.

Other people can be excellent props for adding that touch of reality to your photographs.

CHAPTER X

Lighting

The simplest form of lighting is what I use for my studio work because it is very flattering to women and children and—with a slight modification—it works equally well with men. It consists of two umbrellas (soft boxes work just as well) with one high and one low or sometimes the high one will be moved slightly to one side of the camera. When I move this top light, I watch the play of light on the face very carefully to see what effect it has.

The two lights I use on the front of the subject are usually used at the same power, although I sometimes increase the top one by a half stop for a tiny bit of differentiation between the main and the fill. These two create the front light, the main light that reveals the subject. It is essentially a flat lighting and it will look flat unless you do several things to jazz it up. One is to select models with perfect features that are flattered by this type of light, and I can't always do that, can you?

The other is to increase apparent contrast by using a contrasting makeup, and this is easier to do. The makeup artist is instructed to increase contrast by darkening the dark areas and lightening the light areas when she applies the cosmetics. It's a very simple way to increase the apparent contrast and it almost always enhances the look of the model, too.

I may use other forms of lighting if I am working with a really superb looking woman and I want to do something stunningly different. I may pull the top bank light off to one side to create shadows that add mystery or glamour, and I may add a fill board to that set-up. The side lighting is also used with men to

get a more ruggedly masculine look in their photos. You don't want to use too soft a light with men because it creates an effeminate effect.

I may make a ring lighting by using three silver umbrellas positioned in a circle so that when I shoot through the tiny opening where the umbrellas meet, the light makes a brilliant ring around the face. It's a lovely effect with the right face.

I also use a hair light which is a two by three foot soft box hanging from the ceiling. It has a grid that directs the light straight down so none of it hits the lens, but I position it slightly behind the subject and tilt it a few degrees forward. This causes the light to strike the back of the forehead or into the lens.

What is the advantage of this sort of hair light over the more conventional spot or parabolic reflector? Remember that I am shooting models, not portraits, which are essentially immobile and static. The model must be free to move about with quite of bit of freedom. With the spread of light from this gridded soft box, she can move several feet left or right or slightly forward or backward and the hair and shoulders will always be adequately lighted and separated from the background. It's one more step in making the photography of models as foolproof as I can.

When you use a spot or parabolic reflector as a hair light, it has to be moved every time the model moves and that's a real pain when you're working with models. Perhaps if I had an unpaid assistant to stand at the light and keep it pointed at the model every time she moved...? No, I think I'll stick with my present set-up.

When I am using dark background paper I like to shoot some light right in the middle so the color is several shades lighter in the center behind the model and fades off toward the edges. It's a sort of automatic burning in of the corners without any more trouble than squirting some light in the middle of the scene.

Occasionally I may use fill boards to back up the lights, such as when I have to shoot costumes with lots of sequins. Sequins are like tiny parabolic mirrors that reflect whatever is in front of them. If you shoot a sequined costume

in a normal shooting room, the room is what is reflected in the tiny mirrors. Since the room behind the lights is dark compared to the lights, the sequins will reflect mostly black with a few specular highlights where the flash units are. I avoid this blackened look by positioning fill boards behind the lights; then the whiteness of the boards is what is reflected from the sequins and the glitter of the costumes is accentuated.

I make these fill boards from 4' x 8' Fomecore sheets that sell for $12 each. I tape two of them together along the eight foot dimension so if I open them slightly, one acts as a stand for the other. If I want more fill, I can open them almost completely into a shallow vee shape which will also stand with no additional support, but will form an 8' x 8' reflector. I position them directly behind the lights so they are illuminated by the spill-over from the lights. Then the sequins will reflect this 8' x 8' mass of white card and thus look bright and colorful.

My lights are by Balcar and I have 3200 watt-seconds, six heads, and a control box that doubles as a portable power pack. This outfit costs more than $4000 and I don't need it all when I photograph models. But when I do big set commercial photography, I'll probably need every bit of that power, perhaps even more, which means I have to rent additional lights to do the job. But you don't need nearly that much and if your budget is small, remember that the only difference between my Balcar outfit and an $80 flash running off four

AA cells is the power and the number of accessories available.

A clever person can make do with a lot less light and power if he uses his head for something more than a hat rack. I didn't have 3200 watts when I started, nor do most photographers who work with models. I had a used portrait lighting set-up that worked fine until I had enough money to become dissatisfied with it and upgrade to the Balcar.

Incidentally, I bought Balcar because of the tremendous number of accessories and the way they increase its versatility. For instance, when I bought it, I think it was the only lighting unit that offered grid attachments for the lights.

These are very, very useful and they were probably the deciding factor in my purchase of the Balcar. Today there is a much wider choice, so check 'em all out before you buy anything.

Don't, however, try to save money by using incandescent lighting. It is too hot working under them and you'll fry your models. Stick with flash; it is the professional light today and you are expected to have it.

Here's one more lighting effect you can do with the grid attachments. It's the sort of effect that will build your reputation as an innovator and someone who knows how to keep up with the latest trends.

The effect is of a normally lighted scene, with your model in the middle of it with her face spot lighted about a full stop brighter. You get this effect by setting up your general lighting, then adding a very tight grid to one of your parabolic lights and positioning it so it hits just the face. Use your meter to determine the exposure for the face and you'll have a photograph that will get you talked about. Art directors like to know who the photographers are that can do these striking things and they will often send you work just because you can do them, even if the effect is not needed for the present job.

Keep your lighting simple (except when you're working for a special effect) so you don't have to worry about it when you're in the midst of a session. Learn to set up your lights so one set-up will suffice for a number of shots and life will be a lot easier for you and you'll be able to concentrate more fully on the model and your pictures will be better.

CHAPTER XI

Fill Flash

One of my favorite subjects is the use of flash—usually electronic flash—to balance the contrast between sunlight and shadow. This is called "fill flash." As you know, if you take a photograph in bright sunlight, the contrast between the sunlit areas and those in shadow is too great to record both extremes properly on color film. And, it can only be done on b/w by overexposing the film, then underdeveloping it. This is done at a sacrifice of fine modeling and middle tones throughout the scene.

There are several ways to overcome this contrast. You can reduce the harshness of the full-strength sun by using what the movie industry calls a "scrim," a translucent screen of fabric or plastic that is interposed between the sun and your subject. A plastic shower curtain without pattern would be good for this. It is also necessary to take along a crew to hold this over your subject and move it from place to place.

A second way is to add light to the shadows by using reflectors. This is also common to the movies. If you have ever watched professional cinematographers at work, you have certainly noticed dozens of reflectors positioned around the set to squirt light into the shadows on the hero's face. These are usually fairly brilliant reflectors made of foil on a hard surface. If you use reflectors, you may opt for a softer one such as a white card. This is important if you are working alone; the brilliant ones have to be adjusted every few minutes as the sun moves, while a softer one can stay where you first position it for quite a while.

Another problem with reflectors when you're working by yourself is that the reflector must usually be set on the ground which produces an unnatural

Flash fill makes sunlit portraits an easy, no-sqint snap.

looking light. Light normally comes from above and when it comes from below, it is disturbing to the viewer even when he doesn't realize why it is affecting him adversely. Those who use reflectors are on the right path in their efforts to balance the light, but using them is just one more step to follow, one more item of equipment to deal with.

As for me, I hate to carry a lot of extra stuff when I go outside to shoot. I want to have just a camera, two lenses and a flash. I don't want to lug a bag filled with reflectors, stands and whatnot which I have to set up when I get out in the field. Nor am I crazy about having to move it every time I change camera position and sometimes when I don't, and I certainly don't like having to pack it all up again at the end of the day and lug it back to the studio.

Some people always position their subjects so they are turned away from the light with the face in shadow; the sun is used more or less as a hair light or separation light. This is quite effective, as you can then expose precisely for the shadowed face. There is still a problem with this, however, in that the backlighted hair is overexposed by at least two stops and probably three or more if it's shiny. But there's a hint of good practice in using this type of lighting even with its faults.

My favorite way to handle this is to use the sun as a hair light as I described just above, but also add enough flash fill-in light to the front of the face to balance it more closely to the hair and the rest of the sunlighted portion of the scene. It looks realistic and the flash adds its own modeling and highlights to the face. As you can see from the illustrations, it has a charm all its own and it is definitely much easier to pull the light range together so you produce a well-exposed slide or an easy-printing negative, whether b/w or color. As for the procedure, it's fairly simple, but it must be taken step by step until you have mastered the technique.

There are two ways to do this. The first and simplest is to use a fairly powerful flash unit that you set according to a test shoot you do before you try it with a paying customer. A good example of this sort of flash is one of the Sunpak units that lets you set the intensity of the flash at a number of different levels.

Here's the way to test your unit. Take a subject out into the full sun in a place where there will be little or no reflection from nearby light sources. Turn the model away from the sun so the face is in the shadow and the sun falls on the hair and shoulders just like your studio hair light. Set up your camera about five feet from your subject and put it on a tripod to eliminate any movement. Then, set your lens as I'll tell you below, set the flash on "automatic" and take a series of photographs using all the different settings your variable unit will allow.

You can use any film for this test, but Kodachrome is so rigidly controlled in development that it will give the most precise results. Keep accurate records as you make these exposures to you can tell which setting works best with your flash, camera and film. When the film has been developed, pick out the slide that gives the best balance of sun to flash, and use that setting on your automatic flash whenever you take photos outside in the full sun with that film. For other films you can interpolate the results. If that doesn't produce 100% results with the new film, you can make any slight adjustment needed to bring it into balance.

Now here's the rationale behind the setting of the lens. It is a fact that in full sunlight almost anywhere in the world, the basic lens setting is f:16 when the shutter speed is set on the inverse of the film speed. That is, if you are using a film with a speed of 125 ASA, set the shutter at 1/125. If your film speed is 500, set the shutter speed at 1/500. If this rule is followed, you will always get an accurate exposure when the lens is set at f:16 and the sun is coming from behind you. Don't throw away your exposure meter, however, you'll still need it when you're not in full sun.

Here's an example: your camera is loaded with Kodachrome 64 and it's a bright, sunny day. If you set your lens at f:16 and your shutter speed at 1/60 (the closest speed to 1/64), you will get an accurate exposure of the scene in front of your camera. Of course, this is only true if the sun is coming generally from behind the camera. As the sun moves around to the side, you have to open up a stop to record important shadow detail. And, when the sun is behind the subject, you have to open up two stops to record the shadows.

Now, what happens to the sunlighted portion of the scene when you open up the lens to record the shadows? That's right, it gets over-exposed. But if you could develop a method of boosting the light in the shadows so you do not have to over-expose the sunlighted portion, you will pull all the elements of the picture into a close relationship that will record easily and neatly on any film you may use. Your slides will be balanced with no over-exposure and under-exposure on the opposite ends of the light-shadow scale and your negatives can be developed normally and printed on normal paper with a full range of beautiful tones throughout the scene. Last but not least, your photographs will be so much better technically than your competitors' that you will have more business of a higher quality than they will.

There are a couple of qualifications in all this. The first is that most 35mm cameras have focal plane shutters that synchronize with electronic flash only at rather slow shutter speeds, usually not more than 1/60. Those that use the vertically travelling metal shutters, synch at 1/125, and one or two of the very latest and most expensive cameras at 1/200 or 1/250. All but the latter are pretty slow so you may be very restricted in what you can do with flash fill. The reason for this is that a small portable flash is inherently low in power and may not be able to properly fill a three-quarter or full length pose at f:16, and if you cannot open the lens any more than that because of the low synchro speed, you're in trouble.

Why would you want to open the lens? It may be necessary if your small flash unit won't put out enough light to fill in the shadows at f:16. Let's assume that you have to open up to f:8 to properly expose the face on your 64 ASA film. That means you have to change the shutter speed from 1/60 to 1/250 to keep the correct exposure for the background, but when you do this, your camera is no longer in synch with your flash unit. What can you do about this problem?

There are two answers to this question, neither of which may be satisfactory for you. The first is to get a more powerful flash, one that will satisfactorily fill even a full length figure at f:16. That's expensive, but if it appeals to you, the unit to get is the Norman 200B with automatic head. I don't know of any other that will do. It puts out five to eight times as much light as the popular small units, but it also costs five to eight times more.

The second answer is to stop using a 35mm camera with focal plane shutter and use a camera for outdoor shots that has a between-the-lens shutter and can be synched at any speed. I don't know of any 35mm SLR cameras that are made today with a front shutter, but there are some on the used market. Kodak and Zeiss both made them, and so did Kowa, Topcon and Voightlander. You are pretty much limited on the lenses available for these cameras. They all came with a 50mm (or thereabouts) lens, but most of them had a limited range of others available as options. Some of these accessory lenses were just front elements, but I think the Topcon Auto 100 and Unirex changed the entire lens. If you can work with a limited lens selection, these cameras are available for $50 to $100 in the Shutterbug Ads classified newspaper.

You can also buy used rangefinder cameras with front shutters and there the sky's the limit. Virtually every camera maker in Japan and elsewhere turned out compact RF35s, and many of them were solidly made and had good quality lenses. Some still make them and if you don't mind being restricted to the normal lens, they can be great for your outdoor shots. Most of them are available as very clean used cameras.

Finally, you can use a larger camera for these shots, a Hasselblad or Bronica in the 2 1/4 square format, or one of the smaller ones that give fifteen shots on a 120 roll. Your film costs will go up, but a careful workman can achieve outstanding, grainless results with the 120 format.

Where should you mount the flash unit on your camera? Above the lens about ten to twelve inches is the best place to put it. Most wedding photographers put it directly over the lens so the shadow cast by the flash falls directly behind the subject and is almost invisible there. In addition, by putting the light about a foot above the lens, it forms a lighting variously known as "Paramount" lighting (after the movie studio where it was used a lot); or "butterfly" lighting (because of the small butterfly shaped shadow cast by the nose); or just "Hollywood" lighting. It is a frontal light that is not flat, but is quite capable of producing very attractive modeling with the right facial shape.

The cost of a Sunpak variable flash unit is perhaps $50, so it's not much if you want to learn this superior technique, one that will immediately set your work head and shoulders above that of other photographers in the area. Not too many can do accurate flash fill exposures, so learn how it's done and get some samples in your book and on your walls. Then people can see how much better your work is.

CHAPTER XII

Equipment

The equipment for model's portfolio photography is fairly simple, a 35mm camera or a 120 model, a long lens for those tight head shots, a big electronic flash unit for those in the studio, a smaller, portable unit for use on location, a flash meter, a Polaroid set-up for checking make-up and lighting, and very little else. A studio set-up with an all-white coved background is nice, but a roll of white seamless in any room is a reasonable substitute. It is, in fact, what I use as a regular practice.

The 35mm is an excellent choice for this type of work because of its economy of operation, its responsiveness, and its ease and speed of operation. It also costs a lot less to buy good 35mm equipment than the equivalent in roll film cameras, and it costs less to feed the beast, too. I own both a Leica M6 and one of the new Minolta autofocus 35's. I use the Leica mostly for my own pleasure, but the Minolta is a workhorse.

I can hear some of you saying, "Gimme a break, Art! If you're a professional, how come you use an autofocus camera?" In answer to that, let me remind you that it was only a few years ago that photographers were debating the need for exposure meters built into the cameras. Today you'd be very hard pressed to buy a camera without a meter, probably in the form of an automatic exposing set-up, because that's considered a necessity today.

The same thing will happen with the auto-focusing feature. Today it's considered a debatable novelty by some, but I know that ten years from now you will have trouble finding a camera without it.

Let me tell you where it shines best. First, if you use very wide angle lenses,

you know you don't always do the greatest job of focusing sharply with them because they have such tremendous depth of focus. The autofocus is always right on the money. Of course, you may never use a wide angle with a model, but you will use your longer lenses quite often and sharp focus is even more important with them. As with so many things, once you use the auto-focusing camera for a few days, you will never give it up. It eliminates all focusing hassle and I love it! And I really love the super-sharpness I get no matter which lens I use.

What lenses do you need for model photography? With 35mm cameras, the normal lens—approximately 50mm in focal length—is useful for full length and three-quarters poses, a 90mm is about right for head and shoulders, while the 180mm is my choice for the tight head shots. There's absolutely no distortion with it, no matter how tightly the head is cropped. In fact, this focal length tends to flatten the perspective slightly and some may find that less desirable than the slight distortion that comes with a 135-150mm lens. If you want to be totally lazy about lenses, stick a 35-200mm on your camera and use just this one lens for all your model photography. The 50mm setting will be fine for the full lengths and you can rack it out progressively for the other shots. It will work fine.

If you want to use a 120 roll film camera for photographing models, I recommend the square format for a lot of reasons. The main one may be that I use a Hasselblad, the Rolls Royce of roll film SLRs, and I find it just about perfect in all respects. For the square format, use the normal 80mm lens for full length poses, the 150mm for head and shoulders, and the 250mm for the head shots. I use a slightly shorter long lens because I own a 110mm and a 2X converter, equal to a 220mm lens. This works very well, so I am steadfastly refusing to buy a longer lens just to gain 30mm.

If you elect to use the new slightly smaller roll film cameras, the ones that deliver fifteen shots per 120 roll, the lenses may be slightly shorter than for the square format, but only about 5mm or so. The main advantage of this smaller format is that the equipment costs

slightly less that the square format, and you get a few more shots on a roll. The advantages are small, but they may be very important to you.

As you know if you've ever priced Hasselblad or Bronica equipment, it costs a lot more than 35mm stuff does, and there are no off-brand lenses to be bought. This is also true of the fifteen shot SLRs. You just have to pay top dollar for them, and that's one more good reason for going with 35mm equipment. You can save a lot of money when you buy it instead of the larger format.

Whichever format you select, and I use both selectively, you will need another piece of equipment; a Polaroid camera that you can focus close to your model. You need to get big heads so you can study the makeup to see how it photographs, and to check your lighting. You can use one of the Polaroid cameras that focus and have adjustable lenses and shutters, a Polaroid back on a sheet film camera—either press or view—or you can use a Polaroid back that fits on your Hasselblad or Bronica.

I use the back for my Hasselblad, partly because it gives me the exact same perspective as I will get when I start shooting the session. It does a second thing for me by letting me know that everything in and on the camera is working properly; things like flash synchronization and the mirror-lens sequence. It's my security blanket.

As for electronic flash equipment, my studio lights are by Balcar and I have 3200 watt-seconds of power. I run most of that light through one or two very large soft boxes which I position close to the camera for a very "flat" light. (I describe this fully in the chapter on lighting, so I won't cover it again here.) I also use a hair light most of the time and I throw additional light on the white background to keep it white. I may also use a background light with dark backgrounds to lighten them in the center. This is done only for special effects.

When I shoot outside the studio, I carry a small automatic flash to fill the shadows (see the chapter on Fill Flash). This is a variable power Sunpak unit that can be adjusted to suit just about any conditions I encounter in the field.

That's about it for equipment. You don't need a lot of gear, especially when you're out in the field. It will only weigh you down and be a distraction. This is one time when the saying "less is more" really proves true, because the less equipment you have to worry about, the more you can concentrate on getting great pictures of your client.

CHAPTER XIII

Labs, Film & Costs

I'm a professional photographer and therefore I always use a custom lab for my finishing, right? Dead wrong! A big part of my work goes to LaSalle Photo, an inexpensive amateur lab that does better work than most of the cheapies. They have a mail order division called Cameo and you can see their full page ads in the photo magazines every month. I send them work when the prints are for models I have tested with. Or if I get work for a model at less than her normal rate, I always promise her a print or two and Cameo is where I get them.

My *personal* work goes to a custom lab. These are the big prints on my walls and the smaller ones that go into my portfolio. I make no compromises with quality on my samples. They are my salespeople and, since I want them to be the best, I am willing to pay for quality. If I have a slide that is a beauty or unique, I may have a 30 x 40 print made from it and pay a horrible price for it. I have an interneg made from the slide—an 8 x 10 interneg—and it costs $20, but the difference in quality is amazing.

If I want an 11 x 14 for my book, I still have the 8 x 10 interneg made ($20) and the print is $30 for overnight service. If I am willing to wait a week for my print, I get two 11 x 14's for the price of one, and this is usually what I do. When I had a rep, the second print was for her; now that I'm unrepped I usually put the additional print on the wall.

I am not interested in doing color work here at the studio because the investment in color equipment comes to thousands of dollars and it's almost impossible for the intermittent user to maintain rigid control over the tricky chemicals. I have labs that do transparencies in just two to four hours and they pick up and deliver, all for $1.50 per sheet of 4 x 5 Ektachrome. At that price I would be silly to do it in-house; I'd have to add someone to process it and I still couldn't maintain the consistent quality I'd have to get.

The normal time for this is just four hours max. If I give them my film at 5:00 P.M., it will be ready in the morning. This is true even of Kodachrome, whether 35mm or the new 120 size. I can get it a little cheaper from Kodak because of my volume discount, but I'd rather pay the small difference for overnight service. The fact is that the client is the one paying for it, as I bill him for the processing plus twenty per cent.

Is it worthwhile going to an amateur finishing plant? Sorry, their work is inconsistent; you may send in a roll and get back perfect prints, but reprints from the same negs may be light, dark or off-color. I don't know of a single amateur color lab that has a quality inspector on the premises. They can get away with it because the average snap-shooter is a poor judge of color and is mainly interested in the fast service. If he gets fast service and Aunt Nellie is recognizable, he's happy.

As far as doing your own b/w, it makes sense only if you already have a good darkroom set-up and are a skilled worker. Otherwise, there are lots of good b/w labs that will be glad to handle your trade. Just be sure they are good. There are some that are not, so ask questions and test before committing yourself.

As for film, I currently use Kodak T-Max for both 35mm and 120 b/w photography and the quality is excellent in either size. I still prefer the 2 1/4 image, however, as I can crop generously if I need or want to.

For color transparencies, I use both Kodachrome and Ektachrome. For my purposes, transparency film is better than negative color film because it can be printed or published, while negatives and their prints are ignored by the publishing industry. But you may lose quality when you make a print from a transparency (compared to Vericolor or Kodacolor), so for the finest quality prints, use an internegative to go from slide to print. This is true even if you are making a transparent print, except for additional 35mm slides. I find that when women become working models they want slides of some of their pictures, perhaps because it makes them look more professional. I'm happy to supply duplicate slides for $8 each. I buy them for just $0.65 from LaSalle/Cameo and they are excellent.

If you strongly suspect you may get some sales of large prints from your client (or probably her mother if she's young), it's a good idea to shoot your color on negative film so you can make quality 24 x 30's. Stick to VPS for these shots; there is less contrast than with Kodacolor and is specifically designed for photographing people, not scenery. But if you're choosing negative film for a composite, the new high contrast Vericolor may be better; a print on it would jump right off the page. This is especially true if you use a quite flat lighting system such as I do or shoot any diffused shots. The increased snap in the film would not noticeably increase overall contrast, but just the contrast within a tone. If that is hard to grasp, try a roll of each on the same subject with the same flat lighting, and you may be pleasantly surprised at the brilliance of the tones when you use the high contrast product.

Although I personally like transparency film for most of my color, a beginner with composite photography may want to stay with negative film for a while until he is more sure of himself. Kodachrome or Ektachrome are less forgiving of exposure error than Vericolor. A neg that's overexposed 1 1/2 stops is still printable, while a transparency would be ruined by that much extra exposure.

It's time to switch to transparency film when you want to build a stock file of pictures for sale to customers other than your models. I have built a considerable file of stock photographs that I sell from time to time, so the slide film is valuable for that purpose. This is not a book on selling stock photos, so I won't try to cover that completely here, but here are a couple of thoughts.

Get a release from every person who comes to you for model photography. You can build it right into your order form like all good portrait photographers do today. When the model signs to order photography and prints, she signs a release. You have to call this to her attention or it will not hold up in a court of law, but it's easy to say, "We got some great shots today and I would like to use some of them in my portfolio, so I need a release." Or, "I may use one of

your shots in my next advertising brochure, so I need a release." Most beginning models are excited to think they may appear in print even before they start looking for work, so they sign.

You can also buy pads of release forms from most camera stores. The ones used by advertising agencies are incredibly complex and designed by lawyers to cover every possible contingency. If you tried to use one of these on a beginning model, she would be rightfully suspicious and would probably refuse to sign. The ones you buy are quite inexpensive, just a dollar or two for a pad.

Now, let's say a client comes to me and says, "We want a picture of a housewife in a pensive mood leaning on a chair and we have $400 in our budget for it. What do you have?" I dip into my files of young women and chairs and see what I have that meets his specifications. I find one that is exactly what he wants and I have a release in the file envelope, so I can make a deal.

What I usually do in a case like this, however, is to call the girl and let her know that I have a chance to sell this photo and there's $150 in it for her. Is she interested? Not once have I ever been turned down. The girl is delighted with the additional exposure and the $150 and I'm happy to get paid $250 for

a single print and the client is happy because he has paid far less than a stock agency would have charged. Everybody wins, which is the essence of a good deal.

I suspect some of you are thinking that I could have sold the print and kept all the money for myself, but that's hardly fair, nor does it build your reputation as a nice guy to do business with. Most of us would be hard-pressed to put a price on that part of the deal.

I don't get too many of these deals because I don't have the exposure, but there are a few hip customers out there who know how to cut corners and get more for less. If you can identify them, it will be worth your time to let them know that you have a fair stock of photographs of models that you can sell for less than a stock agency.

CHAPTER XIV

Preparing Your Portfolio

Models need portfolios, but so do you. Your portfolio will consist of big prints on your wall, smaller ones in a leather book, and tear-sheets of ads you have done featuring models. Whatever it is, you need samples of your work to show would-be models who come to your studio, as well as to commercial accounts who may hire you if they think you're good enough to handle their photography. But before you make samples to show these people, you first need the ability to make outstanding photographs, no matter what the model looks like or the abilities she has.

When I began to do model's photography, I took samples into some of the talent agencies and the first thing most of them said was, "Art, your work is very nice, but you shoot portraits; you're a portrait photographer." That didn't seem so bad to me and I asked, "What's wrong with that?" They pointed out that my work was too posed, too stiff and totally lacking in spontaneity, the exact opposite of what is needed in portfolio work.

"When you do composite work," they said, "it should evoke a feeling of action, movement, spontaneity. It needs to be alive, not embalmed like your portraits. Go to the library and look over the fashion magazines, Vogue, Elle, Gentlemen's Quarterly, even Cosmo, and you'll see posed pictures that give no indication of being posed. What happens in the taking of these pictures is that the photographer takes maybe ten, twenty or thirty shots all in a short time span while the model moves about within her pose under the loose direction of the photographer."

I found that it makes no difference whether the camera was a 35mm or

Hasselblad; what makes the difference is the attitude of the photographer, who takes many pictures and keeps shooting until he is sure he has captured the essence of that model or that set-up. The trick to getting the action-oriented photographs the agencies are seeking is to set up a general pose, then keep the model moving through slight changes of head tilt, body bend, hand position, and so on, until you know you have a good range to select from. This is not purposeless shooting like a madman with a machine gun, as some people think. It means that you set up a good arrangement for the model and the clothes, then vary it until you know you have the right stuff on film, probably several good shots.

When I thought I was beginning to take the sort of photographs that would be acceptable to the agencies, I went back with some of my new shots and they said, "Now, these are more like what we are looking for, this is the type of work we want to see."

So I asked if they would recommend people to me and they agreed to do so. Before long I was photographing some very attractive people. They were not the top models at the agencies; the agencies were not going to send their best people out to work with a new, green photographer, so I worked first of all with their newcomers. But I found that their new people are better looking and more skilled than you will find in any modeling school or on the street.

They are good, but not as good as those who have been working for a while. When you work with an experienced model, a really good one, it's as easy as spreading soft butter on warm toast. The first time you work with one of the best, you'll marvel at how smoothly it goes, just incredibly easy. They seem to read your mind; you hardly begin to say what you want next and she's moving into the pose. They know what looks good and there's no hesitation at taking the pose with the best angle shooting. They made me look good when I wasn't that great.

Another great result of shooting the best models is that you increase your credibility with the people you show your portfolio to. The art directors know who the top models are and when they see them in your book, they don't know you were just testing with them, so the way they perceive you goes up a notch or two. And your portfolio gets better and better.

Before I worked with these better models, I thought I had photographed some very attractive people, but when I showed the book to the agencies, they not only told me my work was static, but they also said, "You need to work with better people." I answered, "But these are attractive people and they photograph well, don't they?"

"No, Art," they said, "get professional models." So I began to photograph their new people and they were much better than my previous best ones. My work took a big jump in quality as a result of testing with these models and before long I was working with superbly qualified people, the kind you can't take a bad photo of, and my credibility went right to the top.

Once, in the mid-seventies long before I opened my first studio, I worked for a wedding photography specialist and we had a booth at a bridal show, the kind where all the merchants associated with the wedding business put on a "Bridal Faire" for the brides-to-be. The object of such shows is to acquaint women with our work and persuade them to hire us. There were florists, gown shops, tux rentals, jewelers, caterers, bakers, and so on, including my employer.

There were more than two hundred brides at the show and to be sure they all stopped at our booth, the boss was having a drawing for a free trip to Las Vegas that could be used for a honeymoon. The girls filled out a slip with their names and addresses and gave them back to be dropped in a box until the drawing. The boss took me aside and said, "When a bride fills out the slip, if she's average looking, drop the slip into the box without folding it. If she's a lot better looking that average, fold it in half, and if she's a dy-no-mite good looker, fold it in quarters, before putting it in the box."

"What's the object of that?" I asked. "What difference does all that make?"

"The reason for it," he said, "is that I have only one assistant, so I can do only about 100 weddings a year. Since that's true, I want to photograph only the most beautiful brides I can so that I can have the greatest samples in my albums and on the walls of the studio. I don't want to photograph dogs (that's what *he* said), I want the beauties.

"I'm going to call these women after the show and if the slips are folded right, I can start calling with the very best looking of the lot. After the real beauties, I can go to the very pretty ones, then last of all to the plain ones. When I pull the winner out of this box, I can tell how to select a beauty by the feel of the slip. And that's why I want you to fold them just so."

"If I photograph the ten best looking brides in the next few weeks," he went on, "I'll book four or five more weddings from each of them. If I photograph one fat, plain bride, I won't get any referrals from her because nobody will look at her pictures. Even though I produce a few shots that are spectacular, there's no way I can do it every shot, so I wind up with a plain bride photographed competently. If I photograph a beauty, lots of people will see her book and she'll look spectacular in every shot, so I get lots of business spinning off from that wedding.

I don't agree with the way he talked about brides who are plain-looking, but his business logic was impeccable and I learned a lot from this man about business, things I needed to know before I opened my studio. One of the things I learned from this episode is that a portfolio filled with photos of the top models in your city will do more to get you work than ten times the photos of plain women who are not experienced models.

The moral of the story is to perfect your skills just as fast as you can so you can begin to work with the best that are available. Then your portfolio will demonstrate that you are a photographer who photographs only the best, most beautiful models and it will get you more work than you can handle. That's what it's all about, isn't it?

One last thing. We all tend to photograph women who fit our ideas of beauty, and my idea of beauty may not conform to yours. For instance, I know one

photographer whose personal taste in women runs to short-legged, plump ones with generous breasts. He photographs the great beauties of the city in his work with models, but he likes what he calls "peasant" figures. This man has learned not to trust his own preferences when selecting models and he uses the women considered beautiful by the agencies.

If you want to succeed in this world, you may have to conform your work to its standards of flash, glitter and b.s. When Salem puts two gorgeous people out in a meadow to smoke, they have one object in mind—to make smoking glamorous and appealing. There's a lot of money to be made by helping them, and you can have a piece of it if you have enough desire to do so.

CHAPTER XV

Promoting Yourself

Self promotion takes many forms and the more of them you can use, the faster your business will grow. Advertising, of course, if the first idea that comes to mind and it's the first step I took in developing my own model's photography. Advertising, however, is only the most visible of the ways you can promote yourself and your business. It is still one of the best ways to get started that I know of.

I still marvel at the outstanding response I got to my first little classified ad and strongly recommend that you try the very same tactic in your area, right down to the wording of the ad, followed by a mini-seminar such as I gave. You can book a lot of sittings from that approach, but there are even better approaches to use.

Printed materials figure in most of my advertising successes. One of the best I have used is a small card—about 3 x 5—entitled "Getting Started in Model-ing." I distribute them by leaving them in places where the right sort of people congregate. These are usually bars where the young, pretty people gather to pair off for the evening. I leave a small stack of them on the counter where the American Express applications are, or on top of the cigarette machine with the free newspaper.

I place them in ten bars on Friday nights and another ten on Saturday. A week or two later, I switch and hit the first bars on Saturday and the others on Friday. A few hundred of these cards spread around every weekend usually bring in enough positive responses to keep me plenty busy.

I also leave a similar, but larger, piece on the table at the talent agencies and these draw business, too, although I have more competition on those tables than I have in the bars. You can't do this at every agency, especially when you're just starting out, but as your work improves and you become better known, more and more agencies will accept these.

Along these same lines, I recently came up with a new idea I know would work, but since I am no longer soliciting model's photography, I will never follow through on it. You're welcome to use it.

Here's how I visualize it. Women determined to get started in modeling often go to a talent agency to get advice on how to get started. Most people seem to

think the agency should be delighted to answer their questions, but it just isn't true. An agency is typically one or more women sitting at telephones in tiny cubicles off a central office. They can't assign someone just to answer questions—they don't have the personnel—so the agency will try very hard to get rid of the women as quickly as possible.

It doesn't matter how beautiful the girl, the agency personnel can't waste time explaining all the girl needs to know to get started—it would take hours—so they are pretty tough on her. The first thing they will want to know is whether or not she's really serious about a career in modeling, or if she's just a hanger-on getting her kicks. If she's willing to spend $600 for photos and composites, she's pretty serious, so their first words to her are "We can't talk to you until we see how you photograph. Go get some photos by a photographer experienced with models."

So the girl goes to the table in the agency waiting room where there are brochures from half-dozen photographers, picks out at least a couple of them and makes some phone calls. Eventually she connects with a photographer who makes her photos and sells her a composite. I have gotten jobs that way and I expect to continue to get them that way.

Now, here's my great idea to simplify the agency's work and sell your services at the same time. I thought of it too late to use when I was actively soliciting model's photography, but it's a dandy and I know it will work for you. What you do is make up a booklet—probably with the help of one or more agency people—called "Getting Started in Modeling" or "How to Get Started in

Modeling" and in it you put all the information a beginning model needs to have. It should tell her all the things the agency would like to tell her but doesn't have time for.

It would not have to be an in-depth, heavy-duty book, just a quick overview, a booklet setting down all the different steps she should take to get her new career moving in the right direction. Along the way, put in a lot of healthy plugs for quality photography and your studio, and sprinkle a few of your high quality illustrations throughout. It should list your name as author and offer your studio as the best place for model's portfolios and composites.

Even though it contains a "commercial" for your studio, I know most agencies would be delighted to have a stack of them to pass out to every budding model who comes in the office. Think of the work and time it can save and you will immediately see how very valuable such a booklet would be to them. And I suppose I don't have to say how very valuable it would be in generating business for you, the author. Just be sure the quality of your photography is first-rate before you try this.

Oh, yes. Even though you are pretty good with the camera and models when you put out this brochure, don't print too many of them, just a few hundred on the first printing. The reason is that you will have so much business as a result of the brochure that your photography will improve even more almost immediately and you'll want to put new pictures in the book. If you print up ten thousand, you can't afford to put out a new edition until those are gone, so print just enough for two or three months.

Once you begin, or order composites from Color Q, you will realize that they can also make business-producing, full color advertising pieces that will cost very little but be very effective in building your trade. You can make a two-sided, full color brochure promoting your services and have hundreds printed for just pennies each.

I design my brochures just like a composite, in the 5 1/2 x 8 1/2 format and have them printed two up on 8 1/2 x 11 paper, then cut in two. The result is twice as many brochures for the same cost, so cheap that I can pass them out freely with no worry about the cost.

If I need something in a hurry, I design a two-up 5 x 8 brochure and have a quantity photo lab crank out half as many 8 x 10's as I will need for a particular occasion.

Because the 5 x 8 and the 5 1/2 x 8 1/2 are so close in size, I can use a standard 6 x 9 size envelope for mailing all these items. And I can pass them out freely (because they are so inexpensive) at the talent agencies; I can give them to models when they come in or mail them when they call. If I'm giving a program where there may be lots of models (at a modeling school, perhaps), I can lay a bunch of them on a counter or table and casually mention that they are there to be picked up. This would work at a model's mini-seminar, too. You never know when a passing model may be reminded that "I'm going to need another comp to show my new short haircut," so she takes one and calls later.

In several other chapters, I go into great detail about those women who want be models that you don't think can make it. However that strikes you, it's a fact that you can make good money doing portfolio and composite photography for people who have no chance to succeed. But you have to be very, very creative because it's much, much harder to make Susie Glotz look like a top model such as Paulina.

But it's another fact that if you persevere in striving toward that goal, you will develop great skills in making Susie look far better that she looks in the flesh. Those skills will last you a lifetime and be of great benefit even when photographing the beauties.

Is it worthwhile to extend yourself to get good photographs of the plain and homely ones? Indeed it is. First of all, you have the satisfaction of doing the best possible job you can for your client and that's a very satisfying feeling. You'll never go wrong by giving the client your best shot every time you pick up the camera. The inner feeling of competency will more than compensate for the time and extra trouble you took.

Second, by making great pix of less-than-great models you will gain the reputation of being a photographic miracle-maker, a great people photographer, and that will bring you more and more business. The composites you make for Susie Glotz will have your name on them and when she shows them to her friends, your name will be spread around to a wider and wider audience. Her friends know what she really looks like and they can see what a great job you did for her. Some of those girls will say, "If Susie can be a model, so can I because I'm prettier that she is." Who will they go to for photographs when the only name they know is yours?

All the comps you order for your clients will have your name, address and telephone number on them. The average working model goes through hundreds of these every year, so your name goes out with every one she spreads around, and most of them will go to people who are associated with the modeling trade. That won't hurt you a bit, will it? A lot of my business comes through this one source: "I saw your name on my friend's composite." Even more say: "I saw your name on so many composites I just knew you were the photographer for me." When this begins to happen to you, you will know that you are doing a good job both in photography and in self-promotion.

There are side benefits to becoming well known as a photographer of models and you will find that commercial work will come your way because of it. For instance, when the Chicago Area Cosmetology Association was putting on a big show, they needed someone to photograph the heads before the makeup and coiffure and then again after the complete makeover. I landed the job for several reasons which grew out of my work with models.

1) I was known as a model's photographer and the work of photographing the makeup and hair-dos is almost identical to the big head shots for the front of the composites. The only differences are that the shot is not usually cropped as tightly as for the composite photo and the head is often turned more away from the camera to show the hair better. Because of my experience with models the Association knew I could give them exactly what they were looking for.

2) When I spoke to the people in charge of the show, I asked, "Do you need any models? If so, I can get some very good ones for less than you would normally have to pay." Yes, they needed more models and I was able to supply them at a rate that helped me land the job.

The reason I can supply models for less—far less than the going rate—is because of a "little black book" that I carry with me at all times. In this book is a list of many of the models I have photographed over the last months or year. I don't put all my clients in there, just the ones I think have a reasonable chance to succeed as models, the pretty ones who seem to have the inner stuff; the drive to get somewhere as models.

These are beginners who are anxious to get some credits and want to have more photographs and tear sheets, too, and are willing to work for just expenses and a photo or two. These women are struggling to get work as models and if they are not getting it as quickly or as plentifully as they would like, they will usually take any modeling jobs that come their way even at very low fees. Since they don't have to pay an agency fee off the top, they can be quite flexible about this.

Jobs that come through an agency pay $100 an hour with a two hour minimum, less the agency fee. But what if I can get her work at $25 to $35 an hour with a two hour minimum, plus a free 8 x 10 from each set-up we do of her? Do you think she will take it? If she's not working at near capacity, I know she will jump at the opportunity. I call and say "If you're interested, I have a job at a hair show. It involves a complete makeup and hairstyle and some of the pictures will be in the newspaper. It pays $50 (or $70) for two hours work and you get a free 8 x 10 of the make-over."

Never once has a model refused an offer like that, but if she does, I know the next one will jump at the chance. She's excited about doing it because it's her first, second, or fifth job and it doesn't matter that it's a little job for little money. It's one more job, and she will have a picture in the paper to show her friends.

Every page of this calendar by the local cosmetology association bears the name of Art Ketchum.

Besides, she now has another 8 x 10 or two for her portfolio (paid for by the client), $50 to $100 she didn't have before and those very valuable tear sheets that say she actually worked as a model.

I often get jobs like this when another photographer has underbid me for the shooting. I can point out to the client that he will pay me and my models far less that he will pay for the cheaper photographer and the high-priced models he gets through the agency.

I did exactly that when I went after a dance wear catalog. I asked the client if he had enough models and discovered he did not. So I suggested that I knew

some who would work for far less than the agency models and I would send them to him if I got the contract. I landed the job and I know the models were a big factor in it.

Incidentally, I do not hire these girls, the client does. I call the girl and say, "I just talked to a dance wear manufacturer who needs some models for his catalog. Are you interested in working for $X an hour and free tear sheets? (Yes.) Then send a composite to Valerie at the company and call her a couple of days later for an interview. They want to talk to you."

From that point on, it's between the company and the model. They may decide at the interviews that she would not be suitable for the job, but that's out of my hands. All I did was bring the two of them together. If I can be of service to the girls who hire me to make their portfolios by helping them get started, and to the client by saving him hundreds of dollars in modeling fees, I'm happy, but that's as much as I want to be involved.

As for my little black book, I update it regularly every six or eight months, adding new girls and subtracting old ones to keep it current. I want to have a variety of looks in the book so I can service just about any client's taste. As you can see, a book like this is literally worth it's weight in gold.

CHAPTER XVI

Discovering the Secrets of Posing

Having photographed hundreds of models over the past decade or so, brings to mind when I started photographing models' portfolios and composites. I did not know where to begin in terms of posing the potential model.

You will have a harder time posing models who have had little or no experience in front of the camera, because new models are unsure, nervous, and stiff as an ironing board. On the other hand, when you work with an experienced model, you will find that he or she moves like liquid mercury when the photographer starts shooting. The communication between the experienced model and the photographer is a sight to see. The professional model will move or flow at your slightest suggestion.

When I talk to models who will be coming in for their first photo session, I advise them to spend some time practicing posing. Posing is as important to the photo shoot as are make-up and wardrobe. I advise the models to look at the fashion magazines on the newsstands and imitate no less than 20 or 30 poses showing different attitudes. All of the posing should be done in front of a full length mirror. At first models will feel foolish posing in front of the mirror, but they will gain insight as to their ability to carry off the looks seen in Vogue, Cosmopolitan, Glamour, and Elle, or for men, GQ or Esquire.

Unlike books on posing, I cannot comfortably tell you exactly what pose is best for a given subject. There are far too many variables. Posing is developed

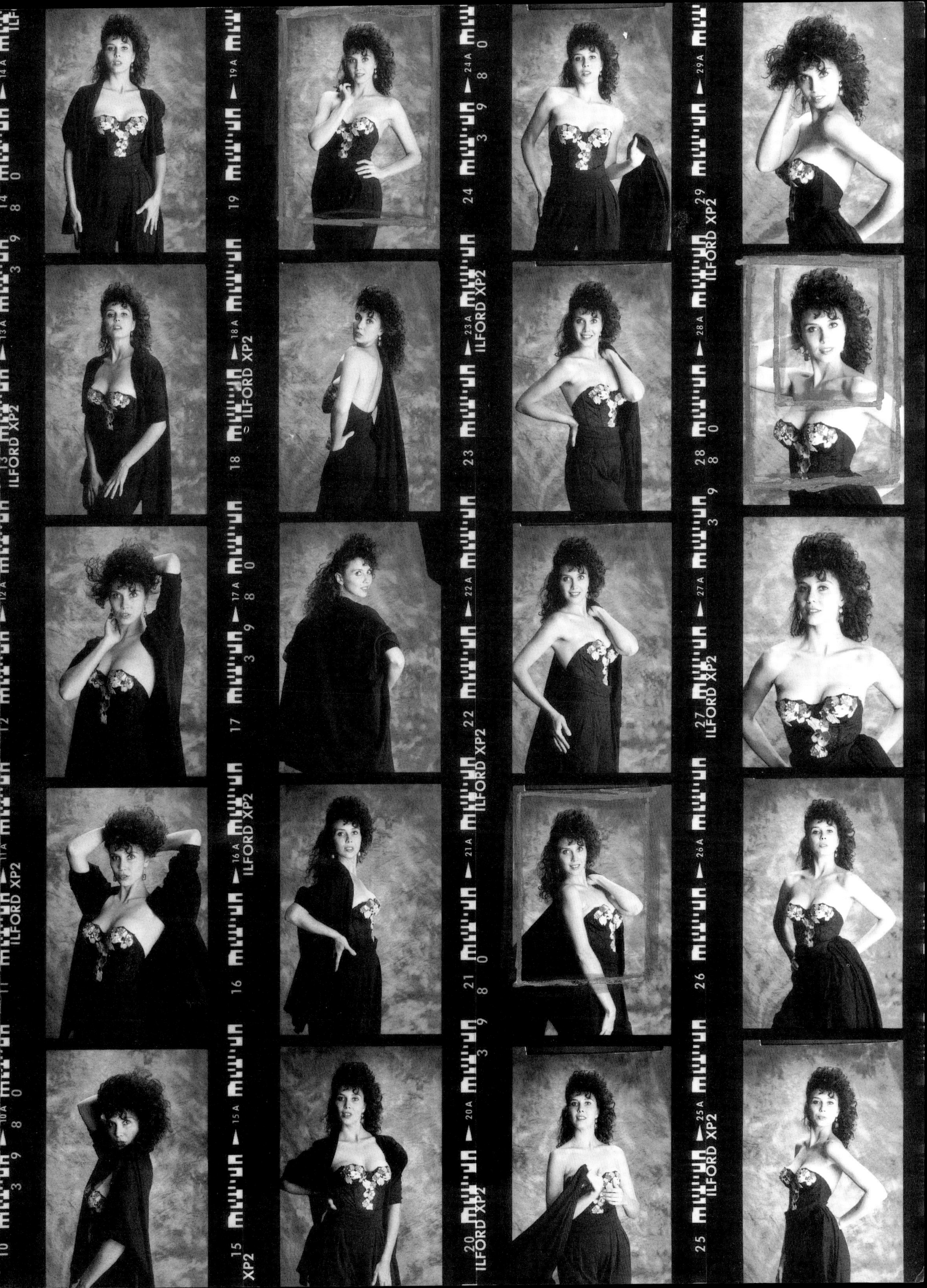
ILFORD XP2

by you and your model through experience and practice. Like anything you try to master in life, practice will improve your skills.

As a photographer, you should review the monthly fashion magazines, look at the poses, and ask yourself if you can improve upon any of the given images. If you feel that you and your model could have done the photo better, then practice and do it. Show the model you are photographing the pose in the magazine and discuss how you want o improve upon it. Try the new idea with your model. Deriving your idea or pose from someone else is not plagiarism. There is no such thing as an original idea. All ideas and thoughts come from other ideas which are improved upon to create a new idea.

Showing you hundreds of poses as I have seen them in posing books seems ridiculous to me. How could anyone be expected to remember hundreds or thousands of poses? Also, a pose that is right for one model could be totally wrong for another model. There are too many variables. The model's outfit, facial structure, attitude, and level of professionalism, along with lighting, and the photographer's abilities, mean that there are no hard, fast rules for posing.

Where do I begin when I photograph that new model? I start by studying other images on composites sent to me from talent agencies or the fashion magazines. Then I choose and start with a few poses that I think the model will be able to do, and begin to vary the head angles, expressions, body language, camera angles, and body tilts. Begin by duplicating the pose, and again see if you can improve upon it. I don't stop for each pose. I talk my model through the shooting, telling her to give me more smile, less smile, turn to the left, turn right, lean, throw the hair and in 60 seconds we have shot 15 photos. If you stop for each new variation in pose your pictures will look posed without much action, more like portraits.

Photographing models with confidence and directing them through their first session is an important step in giving your models confidence and an understanding of modeling. To keep your models relaxed when you shoot composites or portfolios, keep shooting and talking to your model as you shoot. Other photographers find that shooting the model with an empty camera for the first roll is advantageous, since it lets the model loosen up and become comfortable with the camera. Model composite and fashion photography is very different from portrait photography. When shooting a portrait, the photographer puts the subject into a pose, adjusts the camera and lighting, and asks the model to hold the pose until the picture is taken. The photographer will choose the next pose, and after 6 to 12 poses, the portrait shooting is complete in approximately 30 minutes to an hour. This process works fine for portrait photography, but it won't work well for model composite photography.

In shooting the model I find that 35mm works better than medium format. The model needs 5x7 or 8x10 prints, not wall hangings. I find that using my Pentax LX with auto winder and two or three lenses is fast, and lets me keep shooting without taking the camera from my eye. The winder is a necessary part of my equipment because it keeps the flow of the shooting going. I set up the lighting and choose an appropriate background, pick the lens I will start with, and look for a pose that I feel will convey the message we are trying to put on film. An example would be if my model comes out with a sporty outfit, the image should be fun-looking, with lots of action. I talk to my models while shooting, telling them they look fantastic to give them confidence. When the model changes into a pose that looks good, I constantly use adjectives like great, beautiful, fantastic, super, etc. to show how pleased I am with their ability in front of my camera. About a third or half the way through the roll, I may change lenses to do some tight head shots or switch from mid-length to full-length poses.

I run a roll of 36 exposure, either B&W or color depending on what the model requires and shoot all 36 exposures in about ten to fifteen minutes. I then tell the model to go back to the dressing room to change into the next outfit, vary the hair style, and make corrections in make-up to best show the next outfit.

When I send the film to the lab for processing, I request develop and proof sheet, not 3x5 prints. The proof sheet lets me compare all shots at a glance, and I inspect the images with a lupe (small magnifier) to choose the best images for pose, mood, and attitude and mark the proof sheet accordingly. I let the model make the final selection.

When I receive the finished proof sheet, I often find things I didn't notice during the shooting. I look for the same things in the proof sheets that I did when I photographed the model: action and spontaneity, **not** poses. Look for imperfections and choose the photos that best show your models and their outfits.

Look over some of the proof sheets illustrated in this chapter and elsewhere in the book to see if you agree with my selections. Remember, nothing is cast in stone. Your choices may be better than mine. There is no "right" or "wrong" choice; we all see things dif-ferently. More than likely, your choice or mine will ac-complish the same thing: an-other modeling assignment for your model.

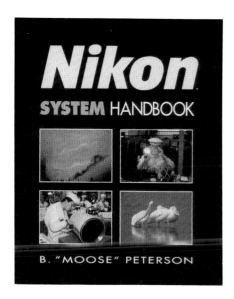

NIKON SYSTEM HANDBOOK.
By B. Moose Peterson.

Complete Nikon guide to current and older models. Lens production and comprehensive discussion of all Nikkor slr lenses produced. Illustrated guide to complete Nikon system, incl. accessories. Includes price guide to all bodies and lenses. **Only $19.95**

THE PHOTOGRAPHER'S BUSINESS AND LEGAL HANDBOOK. By Leonard Duboff, lawyer.

How do you protect yourself legally as a photographer? What you don't know can hurt you. This new authoritative book deals with copyright, your rights, tax tips, legal forms, contracts, reproduction fee prices, etc. **Only $18.95**

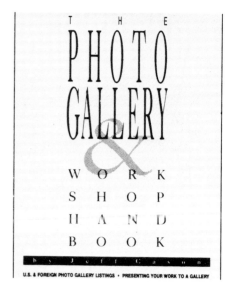

THE PHOTO GALLERY AND WORKSHOP HANDBOOK. By Jeff Cason.

U.S. & International gallery guide and workshop directory. Detailed listings, interviews w/ gallery and workshop directors, photo investing, price guides of collectible photo art, auctions, and how to present your photographs to galleries. **Only $19.95**

WINNING PHOTO CONTESTS.
By Jeanne Stallman.

Your guide to entering and cashing in on contests of all kinds. Included are:
• Prize-winning photos from various contests.
• Detailed contest listings with information on entry requirements and awards.
• Interviews with judges and prize winners.
• Advice on graphic impact, timing, composition, and color.
Expert advice is offered to the reader on:
• Finding the right contest for your photos.
• How to make your entry stand out.
• Model releases.
• Editing and presentation of photos.
• Contests to avoid.

Only $14.95

THE PHOTOMARKETING HANDBOOK - THIRD EDITION. By Jeff Cason

• Detailed market listings, publishers, paper product companies, domestic and foreign agencies, telling you exactly what editors and agents are looking for.
• In depth profiles with professional photographers, editors and agents, telling you what it takes to succeed.
• Sample business forms, photographer-agency agreement, and book publishing contracts.
• Newspaper listings worldwide.
• Reproduction fee chart.
• Color pages from photo agency catalogs worldwide
• 302 pp. 8¹/₂ x 11

Only $21.95

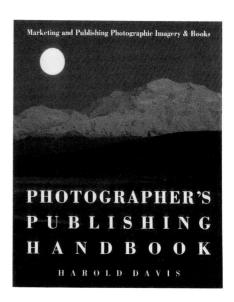

PHOTOGRAPHER'S PUBLISHING HANDBOOK.
By Harold Davis.

Comprehensive reference on all aspects of publishing photographic imagery, including photo books and paper products. How to:
• Create publishable imagery.
• Publish self-promotion pieces.
• Market stock photos to publishers.
• Self-publish.
• Create a reputation as a photographer.

Only $19.95